Everything Will Work Out In the Long Run

by Dave Urwin

First published in Great Britain in 2013 by:

Spiderwize
3rd Floor
307 Regent Street
London
W1B 3HH

Printed and bound in the UK by Spiderwise
Website: www. Spiderwize.com

Foreword by Robbie Britton
(Team GB Ultra Runner)

The first time I met Dave Urwin was in a marquee on a cold, wet, miserable evening in March 2013 during the Thames Path 100, which had become more of a swimming and bog running event due to heavy flooding and wonderful British weather. As first impressions go, I am happy to describe Dave's as interesting...

His cold weather kit that evening was a Brazilian flag and a single strand of tinsel, simply because they were in the same drawer, and it is this kind of logic that puts Dave on a slightly different plane of existence to many but one that makes for interesting reading.

With a finishing line celebration that matches Andy Dupree's at the end of that tunnel of human waste in the Shawshank Redemption, Dave looks like a man who "you wouldn't leave your kids with" according to one long distance runner, but is in fact a very determined, funny and friendly individual that you tend to find throughout the world of ultra running with a past unknown, but intriguing, hence the book.

In the modern age of blogging and self-publication there are many who churn out thousands of words to describe every waking thought throughout their day but very few people who write in the comical and engaging way that this chap does. I look forward to reading this book as much as I do anything that Dave takes the time to put down on paper.

If everyone could celebrate like Dave does then the world would be a better place.

Robbie Britton placed 17th overall in the 2013 World 24 hour championships, running nearly 150 miles. He has won both the North Downs Way and South Downs Way 100 races, and placed highly in many other ultramarathons, including the Spartathlon.

For Boldebort

You have a book dedicated to you.
Feeling flush?

Introduction

Imagine, if you will, these three scenes......

I have just run 26 miles. My quad muscles are on fire and are shooting torrents of pain with every step, and I am feeling nauseous and slightly dizzy. I still have 36 miles to go, and the clock is ticking. I am beginning to think this is going to be a very long day.

I drank an absurd amount of alcohol on a near empty stomach the previous night. I have spent much of the afternoon driving home, feeling more and more unwell the whole journey. Several miles from home I feel myself burning up from the inside, and am becoming short of breath. This is after months, or you could say a few years, of living an extremely unhealthy lifestyle and becoming more and more disillusioned with the way my life is turning out. I pull over and then get out of my car. My head is spinning and pins and needles are shooting down both arms. I am terrified, and am frantically trying to work out whether or not I need to call an ambulance.

I am desperately fighting to maintain a tenuous grip on reality, hiding in a tent that is baking in the midday sun because I can't face going back outside, where I have spent the past eight or nine hours largely wishing I hadn't stepped through the doors of perception. At least if I stay in the tent my world is confined into a space that is small enough to be just about manageable, but it is becoming claustrophobic. There has to be more than this. I look into a shaving mirror and see a version of myself I barely recognise, face twisted in terror.

These are three scenarios from my life so far that I believe are interconnected. In the following pages I will fill in the rest of the story. Not the entire story of course. In between the third and the first scenarios there were over 4,380 days, and a fair few more than that beforehand that equally shaped what followed. If I was to describe each of those days in minute detail it would take longer than it took to live them, due to the discrepancy between the time it takes to think and the time it takes to type. It would take nearly as long to read them. Besides, I couldn't remember it all anyway. It is down to me to pick and choose some of the key points, which if you think about it is what life often is. When you ask someone "How are you?", or when they ask you the same, you're not expecting them to tell a story as long as the one you are about to read. Most of the time it's not even a genuine question, it's just a pleasantry.

I could say it was by not asking myself that question enough, and not answering genuinely when I did, that I ended up in the second and third scenarios described. Part of the problem was also that I wouldn't have known what to do next even if I had answered the question genuinely. Maybe that was the whole problem.

Before we start let me make two things absolutely clear. Firstly, I am not going to tell you what you should do if you are not Ok, I am merely going to tell the story of what I did. Maybe you will find it helpful, maybe you won't, maybe you are Ok; this is what I hope. Secondly, I am not an elite athlete. I will never claim to be, and am pretty sure I know I never will be, because even if somewhere hidden within me is the talent I simply don't have the time, or to be honest the inclination, to train as hard as one has to in order to reach the very peak. This is not a book that chronicles any athletic achievements the vast majority of people couldn't reach if they really wanted to. Maybe you already have achieved similar and more impressive feats. That isn't what it's primarily about for me anyway, as you will learn if you choose to continue reading. You've bought the book so you may as well, hey?

Born to Run?

I don't remember the first step I ran, although I do remember one or two things that wouldn't have happened long after it. I have clear memories of being pushed around the village of Acle in a pushchair by my mum, with my brother Joe walking beside us. There was a dog that would always bark at us and another that would just lie there and let us pat it. We called them 'Wooey' and 'Friendly.' The day we moved down to Somerset when I was two is also permanently etched on my memory, mostly because the moment we pulled into the driveway of our new home Joe projectile vomited all over me. "You've been sick on David's back!" said my mum, and I still have a very clear image of it, as well as of our two cats at the time fighting in a travel box in the front of the car. Joe was also responsible for both hospitalisations of mine during the 80s; the first was when he pushed me off the sofa and I landed awkwardly on my oustretched arm, snapping one of the bones. The second was when there was a broom standing up on its end in our living room and he jumped over it, challenging me to do the same. I tried, but instead it stuck into my groin and I required about six stitches. Luckily though, this was the last hospitalisation I suffered at my brother's hands. We get on great these days.

I do remember showing the capacity to run a smart race at an early age. One lunch time when maybe nine or ten I ran round the school playground 58 times. I was just jogging round slowly, and people kept shouting "Come on Dave, faster!" but I would reply "No, I'm doing a lot of laps." The school playground wasn't big, and I'm not sure my equivalent pace of then would have enabled me to beat the strict cut-offs of a race like Spartathlon now, but I showed that I at least had the mental discipline to run slower and longer. This carried on into my early teens, when I showed a little bit of talent for the 1,500 metres. Of course if I was to run 1,500 metres now I would run it flat out, it being less than a mile, but when I first ran it 1,500 metres seemed like a seriously long way. Therein lies one of my main points. 1,500 metres is a long way to run if you've never run it before. Running 5k is an awesome achievement if you're running it for the first time, so is 10k, and every distance beyond. Even those who run well over 100 miles round a track within 24 hours started somewhere.

Anyway, the first time I ran 1,500 metres round a track, in a school PE lesson, I saw a couple of lads who could outsprint me on any given day shoot off from the start line and I thought they would keep storming ahead, probably overtaking me again once or twice as they went round. However, by setting off at a pace I felt I could maintain I was soon reeling them in, and I overtook one and then the other within a couple of laps, the brutal pace of their start catching up with them. I couldn't quite believe it when I kept putting distance on them as we went round, and I seemed to feel better and better as I went on. Running 1,500 metres then seemed to take as long as maybe jogging 10k would feel now; new experiences tend to slow down time. By the time I was near the finish line I had kind of zoned out and almost forgotten that there were even other people running. As I neared the finish my PE teacher Keith Henman, cousin of tennis player Tim, shouted that somebody was sprinting behind me. "He's catching you!" yelled Keith. "Full speed ahead!" shouted my friend Darren, and so I sprinted for the line and crossed it in about 7 minutes and 10 seconds. Nowadays I would consider that a pretty shoddy time for the 1,500 metres, but then I don't really know what a good time for me would be now because I never run that short a distance on purpose. I don't really feel like I've had a run unless I've done at least 10k. If I was to run 1,500 metres flat out I guess I'd feel like I'd had a run, although maybe I'd do a few repeats. The truth is though I don't particularly enjoy running fast. It hurts, and I'm not much of a masochist. The way I ran round that school playground was much more to my liking, although of course I'd prefer to run in the countryside given the choice.

It turned out I wasn't quite as good at 1,500 metres in the grand scheme of things as I thought I might be. At sports day that year I ran against some kids who were actually good at running and I finished last. I remember thinking the pace they set off at from the start was insane, and I was never going to keep up with them, so I thought I'd ease off a bit and see what happened. What happened was that they got further and further ahead of me as the race went on, but I kept going and finished anyway, and that actually got me some respect. I suppose in a way it was like hitting a bully back, even if I lost the fight. At least I put up some kind of resistance. Exactly the same thing happened on the next year's sports day, and then the third year I didn't finish last, I faded into mid-pack obscurity, and although I finished before some people that time it didn't feel quite as impressive and no-one really said much afterwards. I guess that's the way it is; outsiders only really notice those who finish at the top of the field and those who finish last. The elites at the front have mostly sacrificed a lot to train hard enough to be in a position to finish that high up the field, and those at the back of the field are those for whom the assumption might be that they shouldn't be there, but they don't care what people think and have as much right to run the race as anyone else. I guess when you're at the front or at the back everyone's watching, but if you're somewhere in between it's easy to be forgotten, unless you give people a reason to remember you, which is why during my early races I would put on a theatrical performance for the spectators and would wear a colourful scarf over my running kit. I wanted to be noticed, to be appreciated. I wanted some kind of validation, because at that stage my validation never came from within.

After that sports day in the third year of Secondary School I don't remember doing much in the way of running for quite some time. I guess I figured that I wasn't going to be great at running and so why bother. I don't think I especially enjoyed it around that time either. I remember my dad running along on one of our days out and me wanting to stop and walk after a short time. "Come on, you should be able to run like this for ages!" he said. I don't think those words planted any kind of seed, but remembering this now I can only think how the tables have turned. I don't think my dad would mind me saying that I think he'd rather eat celery than run any kind of distance nowadays. He really doesn't like celery by the way. A few months back he asked what was in a juice I'd just made and as soon as I mentioned the 'c' word he wanted me to get it as far away from him as possible. Because I don't really know how to end this chapter I've chosen to share another memory that has just appeared. One day during the 80s when we were all sat down to watch Blind Date on a Saturday evening, as many families did at the time, there was a contestant called Tyrone. I said he was a word that rhymes with cat, not having a clue what it meant, having heard someone say it at school and imagined it was just a variation on the far less derogatory 'twit.' I was probably about seven, and I can still see the look on my dad's face now. By the way Tyrone, if you're reading this I fully admit that my seven-year-old brain I don't believe could formulate a considered enough analysis of your character to use such a harsh word to describe you. Maybe you were a twit, but if you were many years have passed now and you may well be a changed man. I just wanted you to know that. No hard feelings?

Perpendicular – I bet you can't remember that

Ok, so maybe I was a little presumptuous in saying that you've bought the book. Perhaps you borrowed it off a friend or relative. Perhaps you may be reading this in a bookshop. Perhaps it was a gift from somebody else. Maybe you even stole it. However you came to be reading this book it's not for me to judge, so let's get on with the story shall we?

Expanding on the three scenarios you read about before, I could pick out countless events from my childhood that they may have had their origins in. I liked to spend time on my own as a young boy. Sometimes I would wear a duffle coat in the middle of summer and wander round the school field pondering life while the other children played. It wasn't that I didn't like them, or that I didn't ever want to join in, it's just that even then I realised that a bit of time to yourself can be restorative. Also, I remember from a very young age I wanted to be nice to people. I didn't understand why anyone wouldn't. I would do anything for anyone as long as they let me have a bit of time to myself when I needed it. However, I couldn't articulate this in a way the other children could understand, and so they thought I was a bit strange. Let's forget the 'what is strange' argument for the purposes of keeping the story flowing. I was a bit strange. However, at first I didn't see this as a bad thing. It was just who I was. Carl Rogers, the forefather of Person Centred Counselling, would say that this was my organismic self, and the fact that my self-belief was shaken over the years was due to conditions of worth imposed on me by others.

I guess Rogers may have had a point because some time in the late 90s, when I was about fifteen or sixteen, I grew so sick of not being accepted for who I was that I thought maybe I should just try being who I thought people wanted me to be. My teenage years had been characterised by a love of nature and heavy metal music, two things that were considered a little 'different' by my peers, and as is often the case my peers responded to something they didn't understand with hostility. I put up with a lot of hostility but one day I just pretended not to like nature any more, and created a character for myself who was decadent and nihilistic. In order to make him believable I had to live up to his reputation, and so I experimented with various forms of intoxication. I was very thorough with my experiments, and considered all the variables, but what I ultimately learnt was that if you get wasted all the time then more than likely there will come a point where it catches up with you and bad things happen. I could have learnt this in school if I'd listened, but what I actually learnt in school was "Perpendicular is another word for vertical; I bet you can't remember that." Well, I did remember it. In your face, Mr Carney.

Anyway, the third scenario I described in the previous chapter was one of a number of scary moments I experienced through trying to live up to this persona I'd created for myself. I made him so convincing that even I believed I was him for a long time. I'm not going to lie, I did have some fun times as a result of running away from my true self, and I believe it was something I needed to do in order to one day learn that my true self was actually Ok as he was. However, the second scenario I described was what happened after too much decadence, too much denial of my true nature and getting to the point where I'd completely burnt myself out and didn't even know who I was any more. That was a panic attack I was describing. It was the first of many, and I didn't know what was happening to me at the time. It's little wonder the burn out happened really, because I hadn't been living a healthy life for a long time leading up to that moment. I wasn't getting my five a day, in fact I'd be lucky if I got five a week, or month even. I wasn't drinking a litre-and-a-half of water a day; most of my liquid sustenance was alcohol or coca-cola. Eight hours' sleep a night? Many a night I would stay up until after the break of dawn and then grab a few hours in the morning, and whatever sleep I did get wasn't particularly refreshing. Perhaps more importantly than any of that though, my life wasn't about anything. I had no-one to love, nothing I thought it was worth staying sober for and nothing I truly believed in. I didn't know who I was, what I stood for, what I genuinely enjoyed doing, and I had no space in which to find out because I'd backed myself into a corner putting everything into being someone I wasn't. What's more, I couldn't stand him, and when you have no choice but to spend every day with someone you can't stand there will come a point where you need a break.

If you need a break from someone you can make excuses. Even if it's someone you live with you can grab a little respite by saying you need to wash your hair, or pop to the shops for a bit, or you need a lie down because you're feeling under the weather. However, what do you do if you feel you need a break from yourself? Well, one of the most obvious ways is to drink. When I drank I became someone else for a while, and most dangerously for me I became someone who I found it easier to be than my usual self, and somebody it seemed was more popular. When I drank the past and the future faded into the background and all that mattered was right here, right now. What's more, my inhibitions sunk down beneath the surface and my life had a focus. Something I could occupy my time with, and something that would stop me from thinking about things I didn't want to. This was escapism.

Beyond the marathon

Anyone who knew me between the ages of around 16 and 21 especially would almost definitely have not expected me to get into running in any way, shape or form. I do remember during the absolute peak of my adventures into intoxication I wanted to believe I would one day grow tired of it all and get into landscape gardening, so I think it was in the back of my mind even then that I wasn't living in the way that would make me most happy. My mate Bob commented at the time "At the end of the day it's only an effing garden." I'm sure if I'd said to him back then about one of his favourite albums "At the end of the day it's only effing music" he'd have verbally torn me to shreds, but the point he made was one I still hold with me to this day. I'm not sure it's the way he meant it at the time but his assessment acts as a reminder to remain humble. For instance, I celebrate all of my running achievements, but have always believed that anyone who is physically able to run could match or surpass any of them if they really wanted to and had the time to make it happen. Running ultra distances is as far beyond the comprehension of many as it used to be for me, but literally thousands upon thousands of people have achieved far more impressive things within running than I have. I'm really not that great at it. American ultra runner Karl Meltzer has a saying "100 miles is not that far", and although I would beg to differ as it is a very long way to travel on foot in one go, I agree with the sentiment.

One thing that strikes me as odd is how guys in my running club who can run sub 3 hour marathons call me a nutter for running ultras, and think that they couldn't do it. Really the only difference is that they don't want to. Like many I used to believe that if you ran more than 26.2 miles in one go your bones would start to snap, your blood would boil, your intestines would slowly unravel and your brain would disintegrate. What??? Why??!! Why would I think this when I already knew of the existence of Ironman triathlons, during which people run a marathon after swimming a couple of miles and then cycling over 100 miles, barely having paused for breath in between? I guess it's because the marathon is advertised as the ultimate test of human endurance, and is the furthest distance anyone runs at the Olympics. It's just not that widely known that anything beyond the marathon exists. I think I may have heard of ultra running once or twice before February 2011 but I guess before then I only thought of it as a theoretical concept rather than a tangible thing. As with many people who have taken to ultra running in recent years, it all began for me when I read a book called 'Born to Run.'

Saying 'Born to Run' is a book about running is like saying life is about eating. Although it may be true it only paints a fraction of the picture. However, if I was to tell you everything it's about then the title of this book would have to change. 'Born to Run' focuses largely on the Tarahumara, a Mexican tribe for whom running is very much a way of life. It's pretty much the only form of transport they have to get around the dense network of canyons they inhabit. The members of the tribe can cover vast distances on foot regularly, because they have to. The moral of the story is that we could too, the reason we don't is because we have cars and buses and supermarkets and online shopping. Our modern lifestyle has taken away the necessity for running. Also featured heavily in the book is the late Micah True, aka Caballo Blanco, an American man who went to live with the Tarahumara and learn their ways after pacing one of their best runners during the second half of the Leadville 100 ultramarathon in Colorado. Also some of the most successful American ultra runners of the era the book was written, including Scott Jurek and Ann Trason. It was because of their stories that I really sat up and took notice. I was blown away by the romantic notion of a tribe of super-athletes living in a remote area largely untouched by the encroachment of globalisation, but it was when I found out that regular folk did it too that the story became personal. Therein is illustrated the fact that despite my best efforts I do have prejudices. There is no such thing as regular folk; only in relation to others. If you ask any person in the world the question 'Are you a foreigner' then the answer in itself is never 'yes.' The concept of being a foreigner only exists due to divisions put in place by mankind. If we are all created equal then why should I only believe that I could run 100 miles when I discover that people with a similar culture to me can?

So many things that seem impossible are only so because we do not believe they can be done. For evidence of this look no further than the four minute mile. Roger Bannister was the first man recorded to have run a mile in under four minutes, in 1954, but once he did it was soon done by a number of others. Therefore, a number of people who were physically capable of running a sub 4 minute mile had not done so seemingly because they didn't know it was possible. Some kind of mental block stood in their way. This, for me, poses the question of how much potential, in so many ways, is limited by our lack of self-belief.

Anyway, when I read about folk like Scott Jurek and Micah True running 100 mile races something changed in my mindset, after which my life would never be quite the same again. It was a 100 mile race, which by definition meant that more than one person was running 100 miles. Up to this point 10k was the furthest I'd ever run in one go, and the last mile or so of that had been ridiculously painful, but when I learnt that there were people who ran 100 miles in day, many of whom had not had traditional athletic backgrounds, I thought that surely I had it in me to run a half-marathon one day, or maybe even a marathon.

Once an addict, always an addict?

I have an addictive personality. I always have. My grandma told me that I used to reach my hand out of my buggy constantly in the hope that she would give me another chocolate button. The first evidence I can remember though was one Mothers' Day at some point during the mid to late 80s, when I devoured most of a box of chocolates that were really meant to be for my mum. When I violently regurgitated them my dad told me that he hoped my greed had taught me a lesson. Maybe it did for a little while, as I don't think I ate another chocolate that day, but invariably anything in my life that has brought me happiness, however fleeting, I have always struggled to keep in moderation. Around the same time in school I remember we were asked to think of something that made us sad. I said I was sad that my brother had £14 and I only had £10. Now, I truly believe to this day that money does not buy you happiness, but it most definitely makes life a little easier when you live in a capitalist society. I should have learnt my lesson then too, but apart from a couple of examples here and there I've always been about as good with money as I have been with moderation. If I could have every penny I ever spent on booze, fags, narcotics and junk food paid into my bank account tomorrow I would probably be in a none too shabby situation money-wise. However, it would be a tidy sum rather than an absolute fortune. I guess I've been luckier than some whose addictive personalities have taken them to dark places because I've never been rich. Often when my compulsion to drink was at its highest I would be trying to scrape together enough change for another bottle of Lambrini or cheap vodka rather than splashing the cash on champagne and Charlie. My addiction could have got a whole lot worse if I'd had the money. The combination of my extreme sensitivity and the fact my parents brought me up to have a conscience meant that I could never steal money without it shocking me into a brief period of sobriety. I did steal a little bit of money from both friends and family to help me get wasted on a few occasions, but unlike getting wasted this never became a full-blown habit.

Addictions come about for a variety of reasons, including a strong desire for escapism, wanting some kind of routine, peer pressure, or maybe some are just predisposed to it. I believe that all of these things contributed in my case, but my addictive personality may have been triggered by wanting to avoid thinking about death. I remember when I first became aware of the concept of dying I was just unable to get my head round it. I obsessed over it for months, years even, and would often come out and say "I don't want to die" just as my family had sat down to dinner, or when I was in the bath. I think I struggled to understand a lot of things as a young child. I remember finding it difficult to get to sleep most nights, and occasionally saying that I didn't think I should have been born, or that I wasn't good at anything. This inferiority complex was something that persisted long into adulthood, and was also I think a big part of the reason I liked to spend time alone. When I was alone I wasn't comparing myself to anyone else, but when I was around other people it was sometimes all I did. As I mentioned before, other children found it difficult to understand why I wanted to be by myself sometimes, as other adults would later in life because I didn't want to explain that I found time alone to be restorative. I felt that people wouldn't understand; a belief embedded from my childhood experiences, as things that lead to a negative self-image often are.

In his book 'Why am I afraid to tell you who I am?' John Powell describes how many people wear masks and hide their true selves, because if people reject you for who you really are then what do you have left? There was a lot of truth in that for me, and having spent a fair bit of my childhood being rejected for who I really was by most other children I decided I might as well try being somebody else.

My addictive personality had revealed itself in many forms over the years. When I was growing up, if I had a hobby or interest I would completely immerse myself in it to the point that it was sometimes almost literally all I would talk about. This included such diverse things as trees, football, ninjas, the army, birds and ancient Egypt. The most all-consuming of these was probably birds, the reason being that my dad shared my addiction. In developing this one I had unknowingly become an accomplice in helping him fall off the wagon. Before I go any further, let me make this accessible to the ultra runners among you (everyone else will just have to find their own comparison I'm afraid.) At the time of writing this chapter, Scottish ultra runner Marco Consani has just run 154 miles in 24 hours during the annual Tooting 24 hour race, which basically involves running as far as possible round a 400 metre running track in 24 hours. To put this in perspective, it is 154 miles from London to Hull as the crow flies, so basically it was a pretty stunning effort and no mistake. The world record is 188.59 miles by the seemingly untouchable Greek legend Yiannis Kouros, but no-one else has got close to this mark and many believe no-one ever will. 154 miles is a seriously good effort. It would take a pretty incredible runner to do better. So, instead of running round a track over 24 hours imagine you were trying to see as many different species of bird as possible in the UK within a 24 hour window. Would you fancy your chances against a team containing Bill Oddie in his prime? Well my dad, Bill Urwin, did just that three years running in the early 1980s when his team of four were undefeated champions in the annual Country Life Birdwatch. In an interesting piece of synchronicity, I think their best score was around 154 species.

Let's be honest, I was well proud of my dad for having kicked Bill Oddie's arse at birdwatching, just as I was when he and another dad named Phil King formed a pretty much unbeatable egg throwing duo at the local village fetes in the late 80s and early 90s. In fact when I completed my first 50 mile race the first thing I said to him was "At last, another sporting achievement in the family to rival your egg throwing heroics." It is still etched on my mind the moment that he hurled the egg he'd just caught in the air after the cricketers who made up the only other duo left in the competition had just seen their egg splatter on the ground. The smile on his face was one I'd fully expect to have in the circumstances. As an adult I've learnt that winning isn't everything, and my parents never tried to convince me it was, but I truly believe that seeing my dad excel at these things instilled a flicker of belief that maybe I would do Ok. After all, if I shared the DNA of someone who was such a pro in the ways of egg throwing and ornithology then in theory I had it in me to do well at something too.

Anyway, he was a pretty keen twitcher in his 20s and early 30s but then the arrival of my older brother Joe and me meant that if he wanted his marriage to work and his children to grow up with a secure family unit he had to compromise his ambitions. Luckily for us he put us first and missed out on the chance of countless adventures that would have been for him like running some of the world's most awe inspiring ultramarathons would be for me now. I guess life is all about choices. The choices we make can have massive implications not just for us but for those closest to us. This I would one day learn myself in several ways.

My dad has never been an alcoholic, although some of the stories he's told me of his college days led me to believe that he was certainly no stranger to excess. He bought Bob Marley a bottle of Newcastle Brown Ale once. No really, Bob Marley and the Wailers performed in Exmouth before they were particularly well known, and it was my dad's job to sort them out with some drinks......and possibly to make sure band members were aware that smoking a gargantuan spliff would not go down too well with the policeman on the other side of the door. When he met Bob Geldof years later he asked (maybe not word perfect) "I wonder if I can add you to the list of other famous Bobs I've bought a drink along with Bob Marley?" Geldof accepted, and may or may not have suggested that my dad may wish to get a move on if he wanted to add another certain famous Bob to his list. Also during his time at college my dad ate some daffodils that were part of a flower arrangement made by a girl he wanted to annoy. He may have had a flashback to this years later because when he'd drunk a little too much at an evening concert type event at the local school he said "Mind the effing daffodils!" whilst laughing, as Joe and me tried to get him home. Apparently about half an hour later he demanded Joe made him a fried egg sandwich but then didn't eat it. He has no recollection of this.

Despite the evidence to the contrary, I wonder if moving down to college in Exmouth saved my dad from the possibility of developing a drinking problem. He explained in recent times how he had a choice to stay up in South Shields and get a job with his dad on the oil rigs or study hard to get into teacher training college. He'd been inspired by a teacher named Fred Gray to take an interest in nature originally, and so study hard he did, and moved down to Exmouth. Of course it's impossible to know one way or the other, but maybe if he'd stayed up north he would have felt trapped in a life that he felt wasn't really for him, and sought escapism in the way I did when I felt trapped in a different way. Instead he moved down to Exmouth and met my mum, Christina Gibbs, who had grown up locally and decided to train to be a teacher too. The first time they met my dad walked into the common room at Rolle College, Exmouth one day with a Deep Purple LP under his arm. He walked over to the record player and took off whatever was playing, dismissing it with a few choice words, and put Deep Purple on. Then he threw a spider at my mum.

What is it they say about first impressions? Well I'm not sure it's true, because they've been happily married now for over 40 years. By the time Joe and me were born they had moved to Acle, a small village just outside Norwich, and East Anglia was where Bill Oddie and his team got owned every year in the early 80s. However, I don't think my mum felt truly settled there, she missed the South-West, and so my dad looked for jobs in the region. It turns out I was one decline of a job offer away from growing up on St.Agnes on the Isles of Scilly. My dad had applied for a teaching job there because he wanted his children to grow up in an awe inspiring, crime free environment, or perhaps it had a little something to do with the Isles of Scilly being a hotspot for rare birds blown off course during migration, but either way he was next on the list after whichever lucky person got the job. Instead he got the Deputy Head's job at Neroche County Primary School in Broadway, Somerset.

When Joe and me got a little older he tried to introduce us to his love of nature, something that had massively changed his life. Joe was more into it than me to begin with but around the time he became a teenager his enthusiasm waned, just at the time mine went off the scale. Booze and birds are what life is all about for many teenage lads and I was no different, yet I was so different.

BUPA London 10k (May 31ˢᵗ 2010)

I didn't do a lot of running during the 2000s. In about 2006 I was into it for a while, and was pretty proud of myself when I could run for 20 minutes without stopping, even prouder when it included hills, but 10k seemed like a crazy long way to run when I signed up to do just that for Mind in May 2010. For my training I was lucky enough to have the course of the by now defunct Broadway & Ashill 10k starting pretty much from my front door. Instead of running short sections to begin with I just decided to do the whole course, running what I could and taking walking breaks when I needed to. When I think back to these early efforts and use them as a barometer for what running feels like now I can't help but laugh. The 'hills' on the course, which are basically just gradual inclines, would have their lunch money stolen by many of the hills I use for training runs now, but at the time they seemed to karate chop me in the windpipe and reduce me to a walk every time. I think I considered it not too bad when I only had to stop and walk 10 times during the entire 10k, but I never did any shorter runs. I would just try and take on the whole 10k in the hope that there would come a time when I could run the whole thing without stopping. That was basically my only intention for the race. I didn't mind what the time was, because I'd never run 10k before and in theory I'd have something to beat if I fancied doing it again. I didn't even particularly like running at this time, and I referred to the 10k as 'The Big Run' after an event in a short comedy video Bob and me had made, in the hope that likening it to something light-hearted would help me to enjoy it.

Ever the professional athlete, two nights before the race I stayed up pretty much all night with my best friend Boldebort talking nonsense and watching Eurovision. Don't know if you're a Eurovision fan, but 2010 was a bumper year, including the heartbreaking 'Apricot Stone', Armenia's entry, which most definitely should have won. There was also an energetic dance number from France and a Moldovan song with a simplistic yet stunningly effective saxophone solo. Great tunes. Inspired, I set off for the big smoke and slept fabulously that night due to the lack of sleep the night before. When I went down to breakfast in the morning a French child called me Bob Marley, and I ate a banana and a bowl of cereal before heading down to the race start.

I'd never done an official running race before, and was amazed by the number of people. I was even more amazed with the free energy drinks and bars provided by Lucozade. Free stuff? Really??? I guzzled the lot, well the one of each I was allowed, and made my way to the starting area. Due to my extremely realistic predicted finishing time of 1 hour, 30 I was starting way back in the field and was mostly surrounded by people who looked like they didn't want to be there, or people who were doing this for a drunken bet. The quickest runners in the field had set off nearly half an hour ago, and apparently some bloke called Mo Farah had already won. I was wearing my lucky zebra scarf, and had some sunglasses on my head, and my aim was to have some fun, but I really wanted to run every step. I would be disappointed if I didn't, even though I hadn't come close to managing it in training.

When the starter said 'Go' over the tannoy I broke into a comfortable jog and was determined to keep the pace manageable, but within a few hundred metres the adrenaline took over and I started overtaking people, so I sped up a little more. I soon spotted my friends Rachael and Amanda from Mind and cheered and waved back at them as I passed them. The rest of the race I'm afraid is something of a blur, as I was just so focused on putting one foot in front of the other and not stopping to walk, but I do remember overtaking another Mind runner early on and talking to her for about thirty seconds, during which I established that she wasn't enjoying this as much as I was and didn't really feel like talking. I left her to her own race and kept moving, admittedly dancing a few steps in front of some drummers before carrying on, but it didn't count as stopping. A few people looked at me like I was crazy. I don't know if they thought I was disrespecting the race or they were just impressed that I had the energy to dance during a 10k run, but something told me they weren't used to seeing it.

A little before half way I remember there being a bit of an incline. I dropped my pace and jogged up it, slowly accelerating again when I hit the top. Just after this I spotted some builders and yelled "Come on, boys!" whilst clapping my hands. They laughed nervously, and it only occurred to me afterwards how a man in a funny zebra scarf shouting such a thing at some burly men may have appeared from the outside. I remember feeling good still at the half way point and thinking that if I could just keep this up I'd run all the way to the finish no problem. I think I may have sped up even more, but I did have time to high five some children as I went past.

"Thanks, Russell Brand!" said one of them.

"Hare Krishna" I said, making some kind of flouncy movement with my arms. I heard them laugh, and then another child gasp "It's Russell Brand!" I didn't bother going back to correct her.

Still the kilometres trickled by, and it wasn't until 8 kilometres were gone and I knew I wasn't too far from the end that my legs started to feel heavy. The spectators lining the road were absolutely fantastic, cheering us on all the way, and I made sure to cheer back whenever I could, and to high five people and shout to someone that their hat was the best hat in the world ever, which they really appreciated. I felt I'd definitely run the race in the right spirit. I'd had a target in mind and had done my best to achieve it, but had made sure I had a lot of fun along the way and hadn't taken myself too seriously. I definitely had a feeling of 'Me running 10k? ME?' as it wasn't the kind of thing I thought a former wreckhead should be doing, but it turns out that a lot of addicts turn their focus to exercise at some point. A number of top ultra runners, including two time Western States 100 champion Timothy Olson, have histories of serious alcoholic and narcotic excess.

As I reached the 9k point my breathing started to become a bit more laboured, and my legs felt like they were made of some kind of weighty metal, although thankfully were not making clanging noises every time my feet hit the ground. I passed Rachael and Amanda again, and as I did I shouted "Let's hear it for Mind!" One of my favourite photos of me running was taken at this moment. It shows me seemingly screaming victoriously while others around me look like they're in tremendous pain. I was actually just trying to get a cheer for my favourite Mental Health charity, but the expression of triumph was real. It wasn't over yet though. I passed the 400 metres to go sign and felt like I'd have to stop and walk. My brain told my legs it was nearly time to stop and so they started to be honest about how they were feeling. Eventually I passed the 200 meters to go sign, then 100 metres. My lungs felt like they might burst out of my chest, rather souring the moment of triumph for any runners who happened to be around me at the time, but I crossed that line and raised my arms aloft, cheering at the top of my voice.

I collected my medal and felt like I deserved it. In fact I felt like I may as well have just run a marathon. How could this have been possible? I ran 10 kilometres, or 6 and a bit miles, without stopping once. How could that be done by someone who once couldn't run twelve paces down the street without burning up and feeling like he'd been punched in the stomach? I was totally euphoric chatting to Rachael and Amanda afterwards, and I think I even told them

I might do the Royal Parks Half Marathon later that year. I don't think I went for a run for months after that, but my celebrations went on for days. Now it would seem strange for me to celebrate running 10k without stopping, seeing as it's pretty much the shortest training run I do. My time of 56 minutes that day would be nothing more than a very gentle training jog now, but that's not the point. The point is that in the moment it was seriously impressive, because it was way beyond anything I'd done before. Should we act nonplussed when a baby takes their first step because one day they will be a grown adult who can walk around without thinking about it? Exactly. Maybe there's an argument for that, but I disagree. Putting this into practice is completely different from believing it in theory, but even those who have run over 100 marathons should still celebrate each one, because everyone starts somewhere.

May 31st 2010 was the day that allowed me to believe I could run. At that point I'd still never heard of an ultramarathon, but running that 10k race helped me to believe I might one day do more.

Addiction – The Birds

In my last year of Primary School I was captain of the football team, because I was the oldest rather than because of my ability, and I was the lead singer of a boy band named the Three D's. Our names were David, David and Dan – see what we did there? Our first album was entitled Rhythm Mix and our most celebrated song was 'Traffic Jam.' The first verse went "I drove round the corner and I said 'Oh no' because there was nowhere to go, the cars were coming round every corner and I could not go straight ahead," before the killer chorus of "I'm in a traffic jam, traffic jam, traffic jam, MEEP! MEEP!" Dan did the meeps, and did a pretty fine job of it I must say, possibly due to his liking for cars, and on the third line the second meep was of a different timbre, to represent a lorry. That boy was a true sonic innovator. I was a bit of a control freak as the band leader, perhaps to compensate for my lack of control over the football team, it being obvious to everyone that another Dave was a far better player. Having the name Dave means that nearly every time I am out in public I will hear someone call my name but it won't be my attention they're trying to get. Most people are called Dave really. Glastonbury festival in the late 90s/early 2000s was a nightmare. "Dave! Dave!! Dave!!!" but it was never for me, and when it was I didn't bother looking round. I think I lost a few friends at those festivals.

Anyway, the band imploded over creative differences and it was at this point that I first started to notice how the other children thought I was a bit strange. I'd experienced a little bit of bullying already. I was a slow eater, and so most lunch times I would end up leaving a lot of my food, and probably partly as a result of this I was pretty thin. This, coupled with the fact that I hated the idea of fighting, meant that I became seen as a natural target. I didn't really stand up for myself, mostly because I just didn't see why I should have to. I could pretend I was exercising passive resistance, and maybe in some way I was, but really I just felt sorry for myself instead of fighting back, and I guess this made me more withdrawn. I had friends, but usually I had one best friend who I spent most of my time with, and that was the way I preferred it.

I suppose on paper I should have been the most popular boy in school as football team captain and boy band leader, but it seemed to have quite the opposite effect. I remember one lunch time somebody made a rule that if anyone wanted to play football they had to knock me over first. Another day someone had been telling me all day that they thought I was going to get kicked during football practice and that's exactly what they did. They knew I wouldn't fight back, just as people learnt in Secondary School. I just didn't understand why anyone wanted to fight. What was the point? Sadly though, having morals doesn't earn you any respect from the bullies, and I never wanted to fight back, so I let them push me around and just hoped they would get bored of it. I guess I showed signs of a desire for escapism then. I remember wanting to change my name as a young child, and wanting to move schools. I don't hold a grudge against anyone who bullied me at school because I've seen a lot of them since and had perfectly good conversations with them adult to adult, even had a good laugh with some of them. It was just kids being kids, but that doesn't mean it wasn't dreadful at the time. I remember longing for the time I would grow up, and imagined myself living on my own in the middle of nowhere so I wouldn't have to deal with any of that nonsense. I didn't think I'd ever get married, because girls seemed to prefer the meatheads. I didn't care though. It didn't matter if I was lonely as long as I felt safe.

I was a pretty good student at Primary School. Both of my parents were teachers, so I guess to a degree it was kind of expected of me, but Secondary Schools can be a brutal place for good students unless you are hard as nails, hilarious or just popular with it. The first and third of those didn't apply to me, so I thought I'd have a go at the second one. All I was doing was trying to fit in, but in my end of year report the teachers mostly said I was easily distracted and didn't listen, and my parents weren't overly impressed. I could say a lot about my time at school, but what matters for the purposes of this story is that I had a choice. I could keep quiet and keep out of trouble with the teachers but not with the bullies or I could make people laugh and keep the bullies off my back now and then but have the teachers on my case. I couldn't articulate to them at the time the complexities that seem so simple now, and so I just said sorry and tried to make sure I did better next time. It was around this time though that humour started to become my main defence mechanism, and one day I would learn that making people laugh as an adult can actually make you somebody people want to have around, so it wasn't all bad.

So, where do birds fit in to all of this? Well I guess around the time I first had the idea that maybe I wasn't the most popular person at school, anything that offered escapism was pretty wonderful. In late 1992 my dad asked Joe and me if we'd like to join him on some days out birdwatching, and I don't remember my exact feelings but the events of the subsequent five years or so make me think I must have at least been intrigued. Many people who watch birds like to pigeonhole, pun not originally intended but very much intended as soon as I wrote it, themselves into different categories. You have twitchers, who often go all over the country chasing rare birds that migrate from other countries, birders, who head out to mostly more local sites to see what they can find, and birdwatchers, who maybe just go to the most local nature reserve and look at what's there. Birdwatchers are disparagingly referred to as 'dudes' by a lot of twitchers, and twitchers are considered lunatics by a lot of birders. You can be a twitcher and a birder at the same time, many of them are, but some twitchers may as well be collecting stamps and aren't really too hot on bird identification. Even when I was a birder/twitcher/ birdwatcher my own opinion was why couldn't everyone just enjoy nature in their own way and everyone get along, but I guess that's just not the way it works for most groups. You see it in music fans with people labelling themselves as ravers, rockers, indie folk etc. and you see it in sport with hooliganism. A lot of the time people don't just get along.

In December 1992 my dad said that in 1993 we would be keeping a yearlist. I already understood the concept of daylisting, from his exploits in the early 1980s when two teams would try and see as many species as possible within 24 hours. I didn't know that people did the same over a whole year. On January 1st 1993 we all went down to Devon to start the yearlist and it seemed like the most frenetic thing ever. Every two minutes it seemed my dad would point out a new species, and the list was multiplying faster than I could tick the birds off. All the way down to Devon there were new birds. All the way back home, because we'd forgotten our coats, there were more, and then all the way back to Devon again. We saw 52 species in total that day, which was 100 less than my dad's team used to get on the Country Life Birdwatch days, but I was excited. For the whole of that day I'd been completely focused on the task in hand, and my mind hadn't wandered to the still deeply troubling thought of my mortality, or what hassle I might be in for at school the next week. From that moment I was completely hooked, and my crippling bird addiction showed no signs of abating for the next 5 years.

In 1993 we saw 270 species altogether. That might not seem like too many when you can potentially see 150 odd in a single day, but those 150 are pretty much all birds that live here for all or part of the year. There are probably close to 200 that match that description, and the rest are those that are blown off course, or just lose their way, during migration. In the 90s my dad and me went all over the UK to see different rare birds that had found their way to these shores. That, and the walks and holidays he and my mum took us on as young children in places like Charmouth and Dartmoor I think sowed the seeds for a lot of my passions. I have always been in awe of nature. Even when I was a wreckhead I would pretend I didn't care much for it but I couldn't totally fool myself. I always liked the raves in the forests best. Twitching isn't the most environmentally friendly thing to be doing, and for me it can take away from what's truly important. Something that's always stuck with me is a story about some twitchers who were looking for an uber-rare wading bird called a Red-necked Stint, and an elderly birder shouted "Kinggggfisherrrrrrr" from across the way, causing them to moan and curse to each other so he couldn't hear. I get that it wasn't the bird they were looking for, but kingfishers are amazing creatures, and to me the elderly birder was the winner there because he had the right attitude and was enjoying himself. I guess that's what we all do in some way, shape or form on a daily basis though. We all have our eyes on some prize, or are distracted by some concern or other, and don't always notice the simple things that should be enough to make us appreciate being alive every day.

That being said, twitching was a big part of what made me who I am today, and took me on many great adventures, allowing me to see a number of awesome places that I may well not have otherwise. One of my favourite days ever still was when dad and me spent a whole day from the break of dawn in August 1996 in the Cairngorm Mountains looking for a Snowy Owl. Dad had seen one on a family holiday to Scotland in 1987 but Joe and me were too little at the time to go with him. I had felt this was completely unfair at the time, but now it was my chance to put this to bed. We walked up from the car park at the foot of Cairngorm with the golden rays of dawn breaking across the mountainside, the utter stillness of the air occasionally punctured by the bizarre call of the Ptarmigan, a grouse like bird that lives in the Scottish mountains, and we walked all morning through utterly awe inspiring scenery, nothing but wild nature as far as we could see. As we approached the area we knew the owl had been seen previously, well I'm not sure anything now can quite match the level of nervous excitement. Life was different then. There was no facebook, barely any internet, hardly anyone had a mobile phone or a digital camera. There were actually meaningful events that people would only know about if you rung them up at home and told them, or would hear about them days or weeks later when you saw them in person.

The nervous excitement slowly turned into trepidation and then edged towards resignation. I can imagine now my dad's thought processes may have been a little more frantic than mine because he knew that if we didn't see the owl that day I'd want to come back the next day, and I'm not sure he fancied traipsing all the way over the mountains again. I remember we bumped into a walker and asked him what the time was. We didn't even have any idea, that's how real the experience was. "Half past twelve" he said, and we looked at each other in astonishment. I guess even though there was no social networking and the digital age hadn't really begun time went a lot slower out in the mountains. All the same we thought that maybe we should start heading back, but we were still looking at every white rock on the horizon through our binoculars just in case. We'd been looking for that owl for hours, and had walked over two mountains to get to the place we had to start looking, so we were even less keen than normal to go home empty handed. Just as I was resigning myself to the fact that we would I raised my binoculars to yet another white rock at the top of a ridge nearby. Except this rock was different from the others. It had eyes. And a beak. "I've got it!" I gasped, and we watched that amazing creature against the spectacular backdrop for some time, showing it to some walkers who were passing through. One of them was actually quite interested in birds and was pretty thankful to us. "I've already seen one," said another, "In a zoo." It made no odds to him that this was a wild Snowy Owl in the most incredible setting. An owl was an owl as far as he was concerned. He was probably a racist too. Only joking.

Eventually the owl took off and flapped languidly over the ridge and far away. Sometimes I wonder if that moment represented the absolute pinnacle of twitching for me and nothing afterwards would quite compare. We topped it off back in Aviemore later with a full Scottish breakfast, complete with haggis, black pudding and white pudding, followed by pancakes with syrup. I remember at another table in that café a man said to his son, who was a keen footballer, "If you get really good you can play for Norway or Scotland because your mum's Norwegian." I wonder if he ever did get really good, and I wonder if his dad meant that if he didn't he would still be able to play for Scotland.

That Snowy Owl was one of 328 species we saw in the UK that year. I mentioned earlier that I was responsible for my dad's twitching addiction blooming again, well you don't see 328 species of bird in the UK in a year without covering a lot of distance. The day after we saw that owl we left a trail of empty crisp packets and Lucozade bottles across the country, well actually they just built up in the car, mostly on my side, but we went to Lancashire for a Black-winged Pratincole, then to Derbyshire for a Blue-winged Teal, and then drove overnight to North-west Wales for a Sharp-tailed Sandpiper. If you don't know what any of those birds look like then it's pretty easy to find out these days. Use google images if you feel like it. Other big adventures included starting a day off in Kent at dawn and finishing in Devon at dusk, and one day in October sleeping in the car by an estuary in Middlesbrough, seeing a Great Knot the next morning and then driving down to Norfolk for an Isabelline Shrike. On our way back home to Somerset that night we heard news that there was an Indigo Bunting on Ramsay Island off the coast of Wales. "We could really do with going for that" I said to my poor dad, who had driven up and down the country already. "Ok" he said, raising his hand, meaning "Ok shut up, I'm knackered," but then it became "Ok, let's do it." He drove absolutely miles again, and then we had to go across to this tiny island, on what seemed like a barely seaworthy fishing boat, as a persistent light drizzle fell, and all to see this little yellow bird that had flown all the way across a gigantic ocean, assisted by some fierce October gales. Madness. And yet it felt totally worth it at the time. Besides, I'm playing down that bird's achievement somewhat. I guess it puts running 100 miles into perspective.

When I look back now as an adult who has been able to drive a car for a number of years I truly have no idea how my dad did it. I guess he must like driving more than I do, or at least have a higher tolerance for staring at motorways, for there is absolutely no way I could do what he did that year without bursting into tears in a number of service station car parks and not wanting to drive another metre. However, looking at it another way it perhaps makes more sense. He had a stressful job as an advisory teacher at this stage, and would later have an even more stressful job concerned with internet safety, and when I think of my need for escapism working in call centres in later years it makes perfect sense. Like me birding/twitching/whatever you want to call it offered him a safe place away from the nonsense he had to deal with on a daily basis, and although I don't think he would have gone quite so extreme that year without me egging him on I know he loved it, and found it all to be as much of a buzz as I did. We were addicts. We might as well have been scraping together change for another can of Special Brew. Except our addiction was far more wholesome and fulfilling. I think. Twitchers are like ultra runners in some ways. Everyone thinks they're mad, except for other twitchers, who totally get it. Same with anything really. Twitching is something else though; in what other setting could a passer-by potentially hear someone shout "Little Bustard!" and then see hordes of bearded men scattering to their cars, as may have happened one day in October 1996 if anyone had been walking by a certain field on the isle of Portland in Dorset. I don't know if anyone was, because I was too busy running to a car with a couple of the bearded men in question. One of them was my dad. The Little Bustard was an extremely rare bird that had been seen in Cornwall that day. We saw it. We were quite pleased.

I loved year lists. January 1st was amazing; literally every species was a new one, and so I could start with a completely blank canvass and was totally immersed in the quest. By February the number of new ones on offer was starting to fade, but then in March the first summer migrants began to arrive and then through April and May there were more arriving all the time. Summer offered a chance for a breather, but now and then some exotic visitors would turn up here and there, and then by August the second migration season had begun, which carried on well into October. November and December were about picking up any winter species that had been missed at the beginning of the year, and then there was always the odd surprise. Basically though the whole year was taken care of. I had a constant purpose. I also learnt the clever trick later on that when the bird migration dries up in June and July a lot of butterflies start to emerge, and then there's the moths. There's hundreds of them, and hundreds more 'micro moths' if the hundreds of proper ones aren't enough. I loved day lists just as much. Every day was like January 1st when I kept a day list. There was nothing I loved more than getting up before dawn and listening out for the first robins and blackbirds, then scanning the fields and lakes, or sea, or treetops as dawn broke, wondering what the day ahead would bring. Every moment from dawn until dusk, and beyond if you want to look for some owls, is taken care of. It served the same purpose as drinking all day would in the future, but it was so much more rewarding.

If you want to make your life about pursuing nature there's never a dull moment, all year round. Do I wish I was still year listing now? Well I had a go at it again in 2006 but by half way through the year I realised I was just trying to recapture lost time, and I never needed to read Marcel Proust's works of genius/works of pretentious, self-obessed nonsense (delete as applicable) to figure out that this can't really be done. Nowadays I still appreciate birds, and all nature, but I'd rather take it as it comes than go in search of it like I used to. Besides, in the 90s you could park all night for free in a service station and sleep in your car, in fact you could do this in most car parks, but nowadays you have to pay to park pretty much everywhere at all times. Also, petrol is astronomically expensive, there are speed cameras everywhere and really I wouldn't want to be spending that much time in a car even if I felt like twitching. When I was a teenager I thought that I'd be a twitcher for life, but I also thought I wanted to be a lawyer, and I once saved up my paper round money to buy a CD by the death metal band Deicide, which I pretended to really like. I was being bombarded with new information and new possibilities all the time. I wasn't living a simple existence in the wilds of Tibet with no worldly possessions and no communications with the outside world. It was always likely I would change.

26.2 miles is not that far

When I read 'Born to Run' the first time I believed every word as absolute truth, and that none of it had been remotely sensationalised. That not an ounce of dramatic license had been involved. Maybe I had to believe it in order to believe that I would one day run ultras myself, because it was full of tales of ordinary people who went on to run extraordinary distances, including the author Chris McDougall. Once I'd got over the initial amazement I reasoned that the characters portrayed in the book were real people and weren't quite as superhuman as they'd come across, but that doesn't take away from the fact that it's a fantastic read, and the events are basically real.

Shortly before I read 'Born to Run' the first time I watched the film '127 Hours', and was similarly captivated by the story. The idea that somebody could be trapped in a canyon for six days and then have the presence of mind and strength of character to cut their own arm off with a penknife, then abseil out of the canyon and hike seven miles to be rescued in a helicopter? I guess it stirred the same feelings up in me that 'Touching the Void' had years before. Joe Simpson had broken his leg near the top of a Peruvian mountain and had been abandoned, presumed dead, by his climbing partner, who had been forced to cut the rope they were both attached to in order to save his own life. Simpson then crawled and hopped his way down the mountain over a few days, just making it back to camp before his climbing partner and a guy they'd befriended had decided to leave. I was inspired by tales of survival against all odds. That will to keep going when things seem impossible. There were definitely times when I would actually wish that something similar would happen to me. Seriously. I just thought something like that would give me an unshakable appreciation for life, and as a nice bonus would give me an instantly publishable story.

I had a dream in December 2010 that running felt easy, and I remember the first time it actually happened. Just after reading

'Born to Run' I had bought a Garmin; a GPS watch that tells you how far you've run and what pace you're doing, and a pair of Nike Frees; minimalist running shoes, and was ready for action. In early 2011 I started running a few miles at a time, then before too long I could run 10k without stopping more times than not. However, one day I discovered the Ilminster to Chard cycle path, and ran from one end to the other, round Chard reservoir and back again, and then I kept going. I kept the pace very manageable all the way, but I kept running until the watch told me I'd done 10 miles, and I felt like I could have gone on at the end if I'd wanted to. I kind of did want to, but I thought maybe I would be stupid to.

Around this time I was always worried about money, and I suppose worried about the fact that I would soon be 30 and still felt nowhere near a place where I was winning at life. I found life incredibly confusing, and this confusion meant I found it hard to be around people sometimes, so instead I put on my running shoes and took off. This became my answer to any difficult situation for a while, and while it can't be denied that I was running away there's also no more focused place to be, so I was forced to confront things. Running just gave me a safe place to properly process things in my head, and come to the right conclusion rather than acting straight away and messing things up. I didn't literally run away every time someone asked me a difficult question, but I always went for a run when I was having a particularly rough day. Back then it felt like this was most days.

One especially hard day was in April 2011. That day I just felt like life would never make sense, and that I would always be held back by the person I was. I doubted myself so much, and this doubt manifested itself in failure. Failure to hold down a relationship, failure to find a way of making money that would still keep me sane, failure to make a meaningful, lasting contribution to the world. I perceived all of these things to be completely my fault, and felt like the only way I would ever be free of this would be if I was better than everyone at everything. Only then could I be free of self-doubt. That would never happen, and so what was left? Hiding in a world of intoxication? I'd tried that, and it wasn't a long term solution. Hiding in any other ways? Sure, I could do that but then before I knew it I'd wake up and be an old man and would have wasted much of my life hiding. Eventually I decided to go out for a run.

I didn't set off intending to run especially far, but within a couple of miles all the upset and confusion had started to melt away, as I was away from those four walls that pressed all of my self-loathing in on me, and could feel the sun on my face, and had an ever-changing landscape going past me in all directions. It was all about freedom. Literally all that mattered was the moment, and putting one foot in front of the other, drinking when I was thirsty and eating when I felt my energy levels start to drop. I ran what was the fastest 10k I'd ever run at the time on the Ilminster to Chard cycle path, and felt a powerful endorphin high so I decided to keep going. In some ways it was just like I had a few pints inside me. It was a similar shedding of inhibitions, singular focus and growing euphoria, but the difference was that I had a clear head. I was sober, despite the massive high I was feeling. I dropped the pace a little but kept running to the half-marathon point, which I reached in a time of around 1 hour, 50 minutes. I still didn't feel like stopping, but I felt that if I kept going without a little sustenance I wasn't used to running this far and so things would probably start to unravel.

Luckily there was a service station on the roundabout just where I'd reached the half-marathon point, and so I popped in there to get some supplies. Unfortunately this wasn't a well-stocked aid station, but basically a petrol station, a Burger King and a Little Chef. I opted for some ice-cream and some 7-up to cool me down, and picked up a bag of jelly babies from the garage along with some more water. I asked the guy who served me if there was a bucket of ice out the back I could jump in, forgetting that he probably wasn't high on endorphins if he'd been working in a fast food restaurant, and understandably he seemed a little confused. I told him I was joking and he laughed politely.

When I'd finished my gourmet feast I started running again. Stopping for a little while had made some heaviness creep into my legs, and this had the effect of slowing me down considerably. Probably a good thing, but each mile after this seemed to take twice as long as those from earlier in my run. I ran past the village where I live and to the next one, then round the lanes a bit. The miles kept ticking by, and I won't pretend there hadn't been thoughts of getting to marathon distance before this point, but now it was seeming like something I had to do. It was a warm evening and I took my running vest off, which I would never have subjected people to normally, but at this point I was filled with a sense that nothing mattered. I was out here, it was a beautiful evening, I had run further than I ever had before and while I was here nothing could hurt me. I stumbled across the village shop and got myself a can of fizzy drink, I can't remember which one, but was jogging down the road sipping from the can and a lorry driver sounded his horn, giving me an enthusiastic thumbs-up. Perhaps he thought I was running from John O' Groats to Land's End or something. I wished I was.

I'd heard of hitting the wall at around the 20 mile mark, and this is pretty much what happened. I was reduced to a shuffle with occasional walking breaks, and suddenly an extra 6 miles may as well have been another 20. It was still nice and light, but I did get a sense that the sun was just starting to dip and the temperature was beginning to drop. The vest went back on and I was beginning to look at my watch every twenty seconds or so, disappointed that I hadn't gone further. I was beginning to find this less fun by the second, but nothing was going to stop me getting to the marathon mark. With a couple of miles to go my legs were really starting to ache, and I shouted to try and get myself moving quicker, just so I could stop sooner. Not long before I'd wanted to keep running forever, but by now I was desperate to stop. I wasn't scared of the negative thoughts creeping back in when I did, because I knew that I was on the verge of achieving something I wondered if I ever could. If I'd trained for months I could probably have run this in a faster time, and maybe it wouldn't have hurt quite so much, but before long I would be able to say that I'd run a marathon. What a difference these about four-and-a-half hours had made. I'd never even run a half-marathon four hours ago, and now I'd pretty much run a full one. How?

Well the answer is that I just did it. I'd gone out for a run to try and take the edge off some extreme emotional pain, and when I'd done that it seemed like a good idea to keep going. Now I'd got to a point where the physical pain was making me want to stop, but I wouldn't because I wanted to reach this most random distance, which was the supposed benchmark of an impressive feat of endurance running. Eventually when I passed 26.2 I decided to keep going until I'd hit 27, and I think it popped into my head to keep going after that and hit 30, but some kind of common sense prevailed and I stopped. I didn't fall to the floor in exhaustion. I didn't leap in the air in delight. I was definitely pleased with what I'd done, but there seemed no reason to go overboard. I guess at this point the realisation hit me that there was no-one to share my achievement with. There were no spectators cheering me to the finish line, there was no-one to give me a hug, no-one taking a picture of me with my arms aloft in triumph.

The feeling of being alone didn't trigger a wave of sadness, but I guess maybe it sowed a seed in my mind that solitude wasn't all it was cracked up to be. I still maintain that a bit of time to myself can work wonders for my stress levels, but the most meaningful experiences are most often shared with other people. That day I ran my first marathon wasn't the first time I'd thought this, but maybe it was when I started to think that being alone wasn't my best option for the future. Things felt safer on my own, but did they feel better?

A few weeks later I did exactly the same thing. I was having a tough day, so I ran another marathon. I barely remember anything about that one, just that it was pretty similar to the first but a little bit faster. Now I knew I could cover the distance I was a little less cautious in the second half, and although it was still a struggle to get to the finish I felt calmer, knowing that I would make it. At the time my counsellor Josephine said she was extremely impressed with my achievements but was worried that this would be an unsustainable way of managing my depression. I wouldn't be able to run a marathon every time I felt overwhelmed by sadness. At the time I thought a combination of 'just watch me' and 'you're probably right', and I didn't run another marathon until the low-key but fabulously organised Somerset Levels and Moors Marathon on my 30th birthday that September. I ended up crossing the finish line hand in hand with a lady who'd stopped at mile 22 to offer encouragement when I was really struggling, and I'd overtaken her in the final mile. As I approached the finish line she wasn't far behind, and I knew I had to say we should finish together. That race had been similar to my 'unofficial' marathons in that I'd set off at an unsustainable pace and then really struggled through the second half. It took me a long time to really nail the distance, but those early efforts were when I started to believe that the only limits to what I could achieve would be self-imposed.

Roots of trauma and determination

Gang-related murder? Survival against all odds? Entire books could be written about these two things alone, but I will try and summarise these two events that in some way led to my running of ultramarathons.

On 27th December 1357 John Beville of Woolston Manor, along with a host of armed men from a local gang who were involved in smuggling and piracy, broke into the church of St. Winwaloe in Poundstock, Cornwall, during mass and brutally murdered my 17th great grandfather William Penfound in front of a number of his family members, several of whom were wounded. Not long afterwards Bishop Grandisson of Exeter wrote an account of the murder in his register for 1357, in which he asked "Where will we be safe from crime if the Holy Church, our Mother, the House of God and the Gateway to Heaven, is thus deprived of its sanctity?"

I have to be honest, my first thought upon discovering I had a pirate for an ancestor was "Cool!", and this has often been the first response of people I've told, but when I read about the circumstances of his death and thought about the reverberations that would have been felt through the subsequent generations of my family I felt real disorientation. What's more, I felt like perhaps I began to understand what may have been lying dormant in my brain. Now, not having lived in the 14th century I can only guess what life was like; quite probably fundamentally similar to life now but a whole lot more real. However, one thing I can be fairly sure of is that watching a family member being murdered in front of their very eyes would have been a harrowing experience for those who survived. What's more, as Bishop Grandisson described, it took place in the church, which had been seen as pretty much the ultimate safe place. What did they feel? Helplessness? Disillusionment? Despair? Again I can only guess. Nowadays I guess the average doctor would have given them some pills to pop and may have offered them a referral for some grief counselling, but I wonder what they were offered then. Did the community rally round and offer them all the time and support in the world in their hour of need, or were they shunned for being associated with a gang member? There are few details available on this aspect of the story, but it seems that King Edward III ordered the pursuit of the murderers, before Edward the Black Prince, third Duke of Cornwall, ordered their arrest and imprisonment in Launceston Castle. They went on trial at Lostwithiel in March 1358, where they were ultimately acquitted, and merely ordered to pay heavy fines.

I wonder if I have met anyone who is a descendent of any of the men who murdered my 17th great grandfather. I wonder if I have run a race with them. Of course they would be in no way responsible for what happened back then, but I wonder if these events had any impact on their life, as they may have done on mine. The second scenario I described in the introduction was a panic attack, the first of many I would have during 2003. I have plenty of hypotheses about what led to this. I hadn't been looking after my health for a long time, a friend of mine had taken his own life not long before, I was starting to question whether I was living my life the way I wanted to. However, I would later learn that there was a little history of anxiety-related illness on my mum's side of the family, and I believe that this had its origins in the events that took place at the Church of St. Winwaloe on that evening in 1357. If a part of you lives on in every subsequent generation of your family then it makes sense to me that when I had that panic attack at the side of the road a part of me was back there in that church watching William Penfound's murder. I was unaware at the time it had happened. I had no idea until my mum started researching our family tree some years later. However, that original trauma would surely have had a ripple effect when William's son had a child of his own. His child surely must have been told about what had happened, and if he wasn't then perhaps he could tell that his father held onto some kind of hidden trauma. At some point the story would no longer have been told, but it was still perhaps buried somewhere in the subconscious of his descendents even centuries later. Could this even partly explain why I had been so terrified by the idea of death as a child?

I went to some dark places in the months after that panic attack. Without wishing to sound too dramatic, when I knew I was ill but didn't know what was wrong with me and was too scared to leave the house I basically thought my life was over. As the weeks and months went by I kept telling people that I wasn't getting better. Every day I would wake up feeling intimidated by all of those hours stretching out in front of me, and every evening I would dread trying to sleep because I knew I'd find it hard to drop off and even if I did I'd wake to another day of nothingness. There were definitely times when I thought I'd never get through it, but somewhere within me was the determination to find a way. I believe that some of this comes from my Geordie heritage.

Literally the night before my brother Joe was born my granddad William Urwin complained of chest pains and told my dad that he'd better drive him to hospital. After a few tests he was told that he had lung cancer, and my dad was told to prepare for the worst. It has to be one of the strangest feelings imaginable to become a father for the first time and then straight away be told you are going to lose your own father. My granddad was wheeled into the maternity ward to see Joe after he had been born, and after meeting his grandchild he told the doctors that he was going to prove them wrong. I don't know if God was smiling on him or if his Geordie temper made the cancer lose its nerve and surrender, maybe a combination of both and more, but after extensive radiotherapy the cancer disappeared, not to return for over 30 years and counting. He wasn't quite the same physically after the treatment, but he never wanted sympathy and he continued to prove the doctors wrong by simply refusing to let it affect him any more than it had to. Ultra running didn't really exist much in his youth, but if it had and he'd given it a go I have no doubt he would have finished every single race he'd attempted. This story is something that is always in the back of my mind during my ultras. Running epic distances can be seriously hard work but if I have the genes of someone who can defeat cancer through sheer determination then hopefully I'm getting to that finish line barring injury every time.

Many argue that ultras are run mostly with the mind, and I won't argue with that. Of course they are literally run with the legs, but once you have sufficient fitness to run a marathon it's basically up to you how much further you want to go. Determination is an Urwin family trait. I guess this was partly out of necessity due to their tough northern upbringing. I heard once of somebody, I think perhaps one of my dad's friends or cousins, saying that he'd rather have his bottom smacked than go to Cleethorpes. Apparently he had to endure both, and this was just how life was. I was lucky enough to grow up in a village in Somerset, and although not everything about my childhood was easy it certainly wasn't an environment in which I felt I had to be tough to survive.

I was never much into piracy either. The closest I got was when I was arrested one night in 2001 with a few friends for having something on us we shouldn't. Mind you, when the atmosphere was tense as the van was stopped at some traffic lights on the way to the station my mate's phone went off and his ringtone was 'YMCA.' I think at this point the police realised that we weren't hardened criminals but just a few silly lads who were a little out of their depth. We later received cautions and were forced to talk to a drug counsellor. At the time I didn't think there was any problem, and so I didn't really want to talk to her. I remember her saying "It looks like you can't wait for this to be over," and I said "You're right." In fact I thought it was pretty ridiculous. I'd had one counselling session before when I was at college but I didn't really want to be there either. I really didn't think I needed it. What's more I didn't want to talk about myself. Maybe I felt a bit miserable sometimes but I was fine as long as I could get wasted now and then. To me it was just a waste of time. Looking back now I can see that counselling could really have helped me if I'd been able to think about approaching it as myself rather than as

'Dangerous Dave', the character I'd been playing up to this whole time.

It is a little strange how these two men named William, who are connected through my parents, who only met because they were in the same town for the same reason at the same time, lived hundreds of years apart but I believe have played an equally important role in shaping who I am. I guess every one of your ancestors and everyone you ever meet has some kind of influence on your life. Sometimes this is obvious, sometimes not so much, but I do believe that William Penfound and William Urwin are both partly responsible in their own ways for me becoming an ultra runner. What happened to William Penfound I believe partly led to the events that set me on the path to ultra running, and what happened to William Urwin helped me to have the determination to set off on that path, and to battle through the low points I would face in each of my races.

Torbay Half-Marathon June 19th 2011

My first half-marathon race was to be Torbay Half Marathon on June 19th 2011. I had, of course, run this far and further in training so the distance held no fear for me, but I had never before set out with the express intention of running 13.1 miles as fast as I could. A week previously I had completed a training run of around 11 miles, which had included some long and gradual hill climbs, plus one pretty sharp one, and was pleased with how good I had felt during the run, but I hadn't run a step in anger since. I had no idea if this would affect me on the day or not, but I was still taking this race pretty seriously it seemed. I'd booked a coach down to Torquay the day before and was staying at a backpackers' hostel to avoid having to drive down on the morning of the race. The only other person staying in my dorm room was a New Zealander who was also running the race. He was aiming for a time of around 1.30, and was in bed by around 9pm, so seemed to be taking things pretty seriously as well. I was so focused on the race that I ended up chatting to some of the hostel's staff and guests until 2am in the common room downstairs. There were around five or six of us but the main two I remember were a Czech guy who told me I'd inspired him sharing some of my travelling experiences and reminding him of his own, which basically reminded him how amazing life can be, and a Dutch woman who could make a tulip shape with her tongue. It is probably more an indication of my immaturity than her lack of conversational prowess that this is all I can really remember about her.

I was pretty lost at this point really. I wasn't drinking, and on paper my life wasn't too dreadful, but like I had so many times I was just hiding. I'd been pouring everything into my fundraising job and into my new found love of running. I still had a deep sadness that was threatening to strike the minute I allowed it to catch up with me. However, for now I was still just about outrunning it, and further evidence of my flawless race preparation came in the morning when I decided to walk the three miles to the start. Well I wanted to warm my legs up didn't I? As I always did around this time I got there well over an hour before the race started, because it was still utterly ridiculous to me that I was even there. I needed the time in order to take it all in, and to psyche myself up, to remind myself that I could actually do this. A month previously I had bettered last year's time at BUPA London 10k by seven minutes, running 49.39. Incidentally, my 5k split had been 24.55, which means that I actually ran a very even pace throughout and sped up slightly towards the end. In 2010's race I had slowed down over the second half and ran the second 5k around two minutes slower. I had made massive progress over the past year, most of it over the previous few months, so there really was nothing to fear. All I had to do was set off steady and then just keep it going.

Torbay Half Marathon's course is over two laps, and the nature of the route means that if you are further back in the field you get to see the race leaders running past. Depending on how far back in the field, this may either be because they are a few miles ahead of you or because they're far enough ahead to have lapped you. I am proud to say that in my first half-marathon race I finished in less than double the time of the two Kenyan runners at the front of the field. I am even prouder to say that at the time of writing no-one has ever been known to run a half-marathon three minutes per mile quicker than me. Ok, so three minutes per mile is a fair bit, but back in the summer of 2003, when my heart raced after walking up the single flight of stairs in my parents' house, if someone had said to me that ten years later I'd run 13.1 miles in well under 2 hours? Well if my parents had said it I would have been pretty freaked out that they knew the future. If anyone else had said it I'd have wondered what they were doing in my parents' house. I guess the point is that you have to remember these things so you can keep your faith even in the darkest times.

The two Kenyan runners I speak of that day were named Isaac Kimutai and Collins Tanui. Kimutai took the win by 41 seconds in a time of 1:05:42, which is 5 minutes and 1 second per mile for 13.1 miles. Pretty insane if you ask me, and when I saw him running with Tanui when they would have been about eight miles in they looked like they were sprinting, but had smiles on their faces like they were jogging in the park. By contrast, their nearest competitor Paul Martelletti, from England, looked absolutely ruined. The look on his face said "Blimey O'Reilly, I'm giving it absolutely everything here and I can't get near these guys" or words to that effect. He actually finished just a couple of minutes behind the leader, and what was interesting to me was that after the race it was Martelletti who had a smile on his face and the two Kenyan runners looked a little uncomfortable, as if they wished they were still on the course and not stood around being stared at in awe by hordes of ordinary runners. As it happens, 1:05:42 is still a couple of minutes shy of what it would take to win an event like Bristol Half Marathon, one of the bigger UK halves, which doesn't even feature the greatest runners. Kimutai and Tanui would run the legs off all but the absolute cream of the crop of UK talent but in their own country there would be probably a few dozen runners at least above them in the pecking order. I understand that running is a way of life for Kenyan athletes. Pretty much all they do is run, eat and sleep. In the UK it's not quite the same culture, and this much was seemingly evident in the way the Kenyans looked far more comfortable during the race than they did afterwards. It was like the race was what they lived for, whereas for the UK athletes the race was what they had trained for, and was the time for hard work, whilst the aftermath was the time to celebrate.

I am pleased to say that I took the Kenyan approach to my own race, but with a great deal less humility. As I crossed the start line I leapt in the air and screamed, because I'd read that American ultra running legend Scott Jurek did it at the start of his races. During the race I whooped and cheered, I applauded a bunch of elderly folk who were applauding the runners from a balcony, I accepted a high five from a girl of about six with a mile to go and acted like it had really hurt. The crowd loved it. Perhaps not as much as they had in my head, but something I've always noticed during races is that the spectators love a showman. Back then I definitely thought I should give the people what they want. I've toned it down in recent times but I still like to let the spectators know I appreciate them being there. My theatrics in early races were also partly to help me stop thinking about how far was to go and just be in the moment.

Torbay is a great race. There are spectators lining pretty much the whole course, there seemed to be a water station every mile and there were a number of bands playing at different parts of the town, of a variety of genres. All of these things made the miles fly by, and I remember the hill climb at mile 6 on the first lap seeming pretty easy. On the second lap, at mile 12, it would be a completely different beast, and it wasn't entirely because I'd run further by that point.

I'd kept a fairly steady pace up until mile 10 and was still feeling strong, but then just in front of me I saw a runner try and take a gel from his partner but miss it and keep running ahead after a brief moment of uncertainty, a look of trepidation on his face. Being off my face on endorphins and feeling invincible, I shouted "Throw it to me, I'll give it to him." If she threw that gel 99 more times I'm fairly certain it would bounce off my hand and fly into the face of a passing policeman, but on that day I perhaps subconsciously remembered how my dad used to catch those eggs at the village fetes and barely breaking stride I made a basket with my hands and clasped them round the gel in mid-air. I then sprinted ahead, calling "Hey, mate in the green!" The runner turned round looking a little annoyed but then as I handed the gel to him he looked at me with a mixture of gratitude and disbelief and gave heartfelt thanks. I heard his partner say "That was really selfless, wasn't it?" and if I hadn't been running a race at the time I'd have wanted the crowd to hoist me onto their shoulders and parade me around Torbay chanting my name. As it happens though my act of altruism looked like it was going to have dire consequences for my own race.

That short burst of sprinting had completely ruined my rhythm, and seeing as it was 10 miles into the race rather than just before the finish line I still had 3 miles to go with my lungs starting to gasp for air. Predictably, this lack of oxygen meant my legs started to voice their disapproval and that last hill climb felt absolutely brutal. I saw a few guys stretching by the side of the road, pain etched across their faces. I didn't want this hill to break me. I wanted to get to that finish line without having stopped to walk, just as I had in my first 10k. I remember thinking at the 13 mile marker that there was only .1 of a mile to go, so I would be at the finish in no time. It turns out that .1 of a mile is quite a long way when you're gasping for air and your legs don't want you to run another step. I was in agony, but eventually I saw the finish line in the distance. "Just keep going, it's nearly over" I told myself. That finishing stretch still seemed to go on forever, but eventually I saw the finishing clock and couldn't believe my eyes. 1 hour, 45 minutes? Me? "Flippin' eck!" I mouthed, well something like that anyway. This moment would be repeated several times in the future in different races. As I crossed the line I bellowed my soon to be trademark victory roar, and was asked politely to move on by one of the marshalls.

At that point I thought 1 hour, 45 was a pretty amazing time. At the time of writing my half-marathon PB is 1 hour, 36. I always tell people that all things are relative. Some of the fastest guys in my running club have run half-marathons in close to 1 hour, 10. They would still get trounced by the Kenyans. Unless you're the world's top half-marathon runner then there's always going to be someone faster than you, and what matters is that you're getting something out of it. I can envisage a time when I won't want to run races any more. I think I've pretty much got as fast as I'm going to get without doing more specific speed training, and to be honest I'm not sure if I want to. Running fast for any distance hurts me a lot more than running long at a comfortable pace does. A 10k race is an absolute suffer-fest nowadays, because I'm pretty much running as fast as I can while I can still breathe, even if I can't hold a conversation. A half-marathon I'll run not that much slower than my 10k pace. The further the distance the slower I can run, and although running fast can be exhilarating at times I know which one I'd pick most days.

Addiction – The Booze

Compared to some bullying stories I've heard I got off quite lightly at school, but thinking about this didn't bring me any solace, in fact it just made things worse. To know that people suffered far worse than I did but seemingly coped better just added to my growing feelings of worthlessness. I wasn't always picked on relentlessly but in a way I found it easier when I was. The anticipation of something is often worse than when it actually happens, because when something happens you can try and deal with it. I never felt like my life was in danger at school, but there were definitely times when I was fearful of going. I was more afraid of humiliation than of physical pain. I always imagined the worst that could happen if I turned round and smacked one of the bullies in the mouth would be far worse than if I just stood there and took it while they told me how pathetic and weird I was in front of a laughing crowd, occasionally smacking me in the head with a flat palm or pouring water on me, or kicking me. Being in that situation day after day at times has left deep scars, which are still healing. Even now I find it really hard to take criticism, and my gut reaction when I can't do something is to think I must be the only one and that I'm pointless and stupid. I can rationalise my way out of it most times, but that initial reaction is still there, and it's because it takes me back to that place.

Nature provided me with some incredible times as a teenager, and the thought of getting out in it at the weekend, or in the evenings during the summer, was what kept me going during the week at school. The trouble was though that my teenage years were not like most peoples', and sometimes I just wanted to be like everyone else. The first time I got drunk was with Joe and a few of our friends (more his friends really) at the local woods. I think I was maybe 13 at the time, and I drank a single can of Hofmeister. It made me a little light headed, but I exaggerated the effects massively, and acted how I thought drunk people were supposed to act, basically talking in nonsensical sentences and running around in random directions. Naively, I thought that the more drunk I was the more respect I would earn. Maybe this would have been true if I'd had ten cans, but instead I had the mickey taken out of me relentlessly from then on for being such a lightweight. It didn't stop me from acting exactly the same way on the few other occasions when I was allowed to go to a party with Joe. Each time I tried to make it more believable by drinking more, and at a gig at the local village hall when I was 15 I remember leaping around on my own at the front of the stage while the bands were playing. Then I tried to chat up the fiancée of the headlining band's lead singer. Luckily for me she was quite nice about it and didn't tell him as long as I went away. I wasn't even interested really, but I thought it made me cool; a pattern that would repeat itself throughout the whole time I was drinking. I always wanted a real connection, and someone I could fall in love with. No matter what I might have said in front of my mates I was never interested in anything meaningless. Anyway, at that gig when I was jumping around to the music I guess I was uninhibited and carefree, but I was also lonely and sad. Another pattern that would repeat many times. I wasn't really doing what I wanted to be doing, I just thought it made me cooler than I was. I had already created a character for myself, and before too long I would get so used to playing him that I thought I was him, and he would even be given a name.

Two major breakthroughs came when I was 16. First of all me and a few friends found a pub where we could get served, and then somehow I managed to find a girlfriend. She was a girl I had got in touch with after a penpal request she posted in Kerrang! Magazine. She would later tell me that around 50 people had replied, and most of them she hadn't responded to because they seemed like idiots, but she exchanged letters with me and a few others, and then eventually whittled it down to just me. The fact she'd chosen me out of everyone still wasn't enough to boost my self-esteem enough to believe she'd want to stay with me. Before I met her in person I saw her in a dream, and she made a face in the dream that she made all the time in real life when

I met her. She lived at the other end of the country to me, in the Lake District, and I went to visit her one weekend in I think about April 1998. I felt pretty awkward around her all day but we seemed to get on Ok. That evening we went out in town and my nerves evaporated as I quaffed back a couple of pints of cider at great velocity. That was what made booze most intoxicating of all for me. Instead of thinking "I can't say that, I can't say anything, they'll think I'm stupid" I didn't think at all, I just said and did things. The countless inhibitions that held me back just weren't there. Unfortunately though on that occasion I suddenly felt queasy and then regurgitated the cider, along with the dinner her mum had cooked for us, on the table in front of her. Similarly to my dad throwing a spider at my mum, my projectile vomiting nearly into this girl's lap didn't stop her from going out with me. The major difference though was that instead of being married for over 40 years and counting we split up after four months. It was partly because she didn't want to be in a serious relationship, partly because I had no idea why she wanted to be with me and told her that almost constantly. Must have been pretty annoying.

At the time I thought I loved her. Looking back now I think I just found it overwhelming that somebody wanted to be with me, and thought I'd majorly lucked out and would have to keep her because nobody else would ever like me. All I really wanted was a proper connection. Something good in my life that would remain constant, on which I could always rely. When this was broken so was I. She finished with me by letter. I'd known it was coming because her mum had said she was out when I'd tried to phone the previous couple of nights, and we'd always spoken every day before that. As soon as I'd read the letter I set fire to a picture of us, momentarily panicked that my whole room was going to go up in flames and then when it didn't I went downstairs and poured myself a whiskey and coke. I'd done the same the previous couple of nights, and I drank every day for the next few. My mum told me it wasn't the answer, and although I knew she was right I didn't know what else to do. I'd spent a lot of my teenage years thinking no-one would ever love me, then I met someone who said she did and she became my world. Barely a minute went by every day when I didn't think about her, and my own self-worth I measured in terms of how much she seemed to want my attention. What's more, a big part of the reason I'd stopped birding was because I couldn't face telling her I was into it. I thought if she knew she'd think I was weird, like people at school had, and so I just forced myself to pretend I wasn't. Now I'd lost both. Of course I could have just gone back to birding as if nothing had happened, but I didn't see that as an option. Besides, I'd pretty much convinced myself that nature wasn't my thing any more.

Birding was my escape from my struggle to fit in and my inability to cope with life. I'd thrown it away and instead invested all my energy and focus into a relationship that was never going to last. Now there was nowhere for my focus to go, and so I drank. I started doing A-levels at Taunton's Richard Huish College in September 1998, but mostly doing subjects I just thought might help me get a job rather than ones I was genuinely interested in. I'd known for some time that my heart wasn't really in education any more. I'd done two weeks' work experience at Portland Bird Observatory the year before and if I'd been offered a job there at the time I have not a moment's doubt I would have taken it. I really enjoyed the solitude, being out in nature every day and then reading or writing in the evenings. I was away from the bullies and could be whoever I wanted to be. It was my first real taste of independence. My second sadly coincided with a new found liking for alcohol. On the night of my last GCSE exam that year I'd gone to one of the village pubs with a few mates and drank about four pints of cider and a double vodka. That was a lot for me at the time, and I ended up passing out in a field surrounded by my own vomit, only to be woken by the first rays of dawn hours later. On my way home I rang the speaking clock from a phone box, realising it was about 4.30am. When I got home my mum was still waiting up for me, which I felt dreadful about, but not dreadful enough to take it easier on the booze next time.

At school, although to be fair I did get a bit of respect for going in dressed in full goth regalia on the final non-uniform day, people thought my being different was a bad thing. At college people seemed to think it was a great thing. I made lots of friends in a short space of time and a lot of them liked drinking as much as I did. I wasn't really interested in going to the lessons because when my relationship had ended I basically felt like life was futile. I hadn't had the nerve to tell this girl I was supposed to have loved what my real passion in life was, and so I'd been who I thought she wanted me to be and it wasn't enough for her. I rejected myself for fear that she would reject me, and then she rejected me anyway. Let's just say I didn't really feel like a winner.

It was also around this time I started smoking properly. I'd had the occasional cigarette before, but when I got to college I pretended I was a hardened smoker and drinker, and I made it true just by doing it. People who I thought would have picked on me at school seemed to think I was pretty awesome, and I was honoured to give them cigarettes when they asked if I had a spare one. I was being accepted by the cool kids, and most days I would go and drink with them. I didn't have much money, but I managed to sell my telescope from my birding days and turned all £300 or so of the proceeds into booze within a few weeks. My social life was fuller than it had ever been, and I was having a great laugh with all my new mates, but looking back now I can see that I didn't genuinely have all that much in common with most of them, and most of our conversations revolved around booze. A few times I spent the bus journey home desperately trying not to be sick, and would find a convenient field to chuck my guts up in before going home and pretending to be sober.

At the time I felt like people wanted me to move on from my break-up before I was ready. I remember my parents wanted to do something for my 17th birthday but I just wasn't interested. I didn't want anyone to know it was my birthday and I just wanted to get it over with. How was I meant to have a special day when I didn't feel remotely special? I felt like a total waste of space, that I wasn't worth anything, and so that's how I behaved. I didn't look after myself in the slightest, and treated my body like a waste disposal unit. I felt that all I was good for was to get wasted and provide people with a bit of entertainment. If people found my drunken antics amusing then at least I served some kind of purpose.

The effect this had on my college studies was predictable. I hardly went to any classes, and I just wasn't remotely interested in being there. I didn't see much of a future beyond college, and so what was the point? By January 1999 I'd left, saying I was going to come back the following September. Now I'd freed up more drinking time, and got a job picking tomatoes for cash in hand pay every week. This lethal combination meant I spent most of my free time in pubs. I didn't learn many important life skills doing this, but I did become pretty good at pool, once holding the table at the Voodoo Lounge for over 2 hours, it having a 'winner stays on' policy and being free to play. I also got better at drinking, although still not good enough to hold it down all the time. I once had jet black vomit after drinking about ten pints of Guinness in an all-day session. There had come a point that day when I'd thought to myself "Right, I've definitely drunk enough now. I'm paralytic", and so a couple of hours after that I stopped drinking and left the pub. "I feel sick," I thought, "But it's Ok, I can make it back to the toilet.....no I can't......but I can make it to that bin over there.....no I can't" and so I was that guy who vomits on the street. Many people would say I was just a young lad being a young lad, and discovering who I was, but really I was forgetting more and more who I was each day and was drinking so I didn't have to think about what a mess I was making of my life. It was unavoidable whenever I sobered up that I wasn't heading in a good direction, so I just started drinking again as soon as possible. I thought I could keep running forever.

Seaview 17 (31ˢᵗ July 2011)

Somebody once asked me if I'd ever done a race in which I didn't really feel like running that day. So far it has only happened once. Before we get to that though let me tell you about the Seaview 17 itself, which is probably now my favourite race. It's not 17 miles long, it's actually closer to 21, and it's called the 17 either because it's 17 miles from the starting point to the finishing point as the crow flies or because it's the race organiser's favourite number. No-one seems too clear as to which one's true. It starts in Countisbury, near Lynmouth in North-east Devon, and finishes in Minehead in North-west Somerset. It pretty much follows the South-West Coast Path, and the race is superbly organised and probably the best value for money of any race I have entered. It's £7 to do the race, and for that you get a bus to the start from Minehead college, a few aid stations along the route and as much free food as you want from a glorious spread at the finish line, including some top notch cakes. You don't get a medal or t-shirt for finishing, but that doesn't bother me. Many people who take part say if you race it then it's a good indication of what your time for a flat marathon would be. 20 odd miles of varied terrain with a couple of very challenging climbs and a fair few undulations make this a pretty taxing one, but the scenery is absolutely stunning the whole way, at least until you get to Minehead and run through the town to the finish.

The first time I did this race, in 2011, I'd had a bad day the day before, when my boss at work had brought up something he wasn't happy with in front of several other people as part of a supposed team building exercise, never having talked to me about it first. One of the other staff members joined in with the criticism and I felt like I was back at school, not part of the clique. When I'd first started the job I'd felt confident standing up to the boss if I disagreed with him on something, but I hadn't been feeling confident that day to begin with, for a number of reasons. I'd had a couple of big misunderstandings with people close to me that were beginning to really grind me down, and my job on the whole was becoming pretty stressful. I had way too much on my plate and felt I couldn't say I was struggling to cope because then I might lose the job, and I didn't feel like I had any other options at the time.

On the morning of 31st July 2011 I arrived at West Somerset Community College at 7.30, over an hour-and-a-half before the bus was due to leave for the race start. The college wasn't open at the time and I was looking around for somewhere I could get rid of all the water I'd drunk on the way there. Nowhere seemed particularly secluded, and I found some public toilets but they charged twenty pence, which I wasn't going to pay on principle. Eventually I found some bushes, and by the time I got back I was able to pick up my race number.

We took a bus to the starting point and I chatted to another runner, mostly about how hilly the course was. When we got to the start there was little time to warm up before we were off. The first mile or so was all flat and downhill, then I set off up the first climb steadily, but when I got to the top of it I was overcome with something I didn't really recognise. Perhaps it was a bit of lethargy, perhaps just a thought of "Blimey, this is 21 miles – I'm not sure if I can do that today." I soon realised that I was feeling depressed, and today what normally helped to take the edge off things just wasn't working. I felt like I'd been punched in the stomach at the top of that climb, and was really struggling up the next few. I'd hit a wall already, and didn't know what to do. Part of me felt like just sitting by the side of the trail and not moving, another part of me thought that if I kept moving I might feel better.

Luckily I soon fell into pace with a Polish runner who had set off too fast and was happy to just amble along. We chatted for a while and the human contact started to take the edge off things a little. He said my pronunciation of the few Polish words I knew was excellent, which made me smile. I chatted to another few runners along the way, and hadn't really been used to this before as I'd only really done road races, where not so much conversation seems to happen mid-race. Nowadays it does if I've got anything to do with it, but back then I would only usually speak during a race if I was spoken to. At least to other runners. The water stations had food items, which I wasn't used to either, and the volunteers were fabulous. A poor huge, bald man got a hug from me for giving me half a banana when I was in need of a boost. Just before the second massive climb there were honey sandwiches and jelly babies, much to the annoyance of a vegan runner who couldn't eat any of it. "You can have water though, can't you?" said the volunteers. What else could they say?

I was finding things much, much tougher than I had during a training run on the course just a couple of weeks earlier. I just couldn't get going for any length of time at any kind of steady pace. There were times when I felt Ok for a little while, but these were always short-lived. The second massive climb was at Selworthy Beacon. It goes pretty much straight up, is not very runnable, and seems to go on forever. I'd had a disagreement at this time with my best friend Boldebort and the day we'd first realised how much we made each other laugh had been when we'd done a training walk here before doing the Three Peaks challenge, so being here just reminded me of how things had changed and I missed her so much that by the top of the hill I was fighting back the tears. Thankfully we would later sort things out, and have been on many, many more adventures and shared countless laughs since, but I'm not sure I've ever felt such intense sadness in a moment as I did then. Everyone staggered up that hill. It felt more like a funeral procession than three quarters of the way through a running race. When we got to the top I had nothing left to give. My determination was shot to pieces, and I just walked mostly with my head down for some time. When anyone passed me and asked if I was Ok I could only nod.

At mile 17 the runner I'd chatted to on the bus earlier was going to pass me but he stopped to walk with me and asked if my quads had tightened up again, as I had told him they had during my training run. I decided just to be honest and tell him I was really struggling with my motivation. What happened next was something I'd always try and pass on in kind if I had a chance in future races. He forgot about his own race and stayed with me. Before long nothing felt harrowing any more, and I said we should start running. We did, and with my new pacer I got into a proper running rhythm on what was the first downhill section for some time. We were chatting away and I was able to put my sadness to one side for the time being. What he did for me makes me guilty that I dropped him when we got to Minehead seafront, but then he had told me to, even after me asking if he was sure and trying to pretend that I had nothing left in my legs. He saw right through me, and insisted that I kept going. I picked up the pace, and very near the finish I briefly spoke to Emma Greig and Lynn Cunningham, who would later become club mates, and a couple of the tiny handful of fellow ultra runners at Running Forever Running Club. When I got to the field where the finish line was I finally found some real energy and broke into something approaching a sprint finish. I was applauded to the line, and when I crossed it I couldn't resist a fist pump and a deafening victory shout, before disappearing round a corner to compose myself.

My finishing time was about 4 hours and 13 minutes. The next year I would go back and finish in 3 hours, 31. My head was in a better place this time, I had trained much better, I'd got faster by running with the club and I'd known the course a little better, so knew when to hold back and when to push on. I went back a third year running and struggled a little due to a lack of recent training and residual tiredness from some ultras, finishing in a little under four hours I think. The second year I was running climbs that I would walk on the other two occasions, and kept up a much better pace throughout. I still feel like I have unfinished business with this race, and maybe one day will finish in closer to three hours, just like with a flat marathon, but I'm definitely happy with all three of my efforts there. It is possibly my favourite race because of the amount of adversity I had to battle that first year. I maintain that once you've got a half-decent level of running fitness it's a more mental than physical battle, and if you're not there mentally running 21 miles is quite a task. I would arguably consider finishing that race my biggest achievement, simply because I could sometimes find getting out of bed enough of a challenge when depressed, let alone running miles along a challenging coastal path. It would have been a lot harder without the kindness of other runners that day, and I've mostly found that this is something that can be relied on. Things may get a little competitive at the top end of the field, but by and large we're all out there to help each other because we're all in the same boat. This is one of my favourite things about running races. None of the things that may usually divide us in life are there, we're all there for one common purpose. How I wish life could always be this way.

Exploring all the variables

Addiction becomes a vicious cycle. It's different for everyone, but many speak of similar experiences. We get intoxicated to forget, then forgetting feels good so we want to stay in that place. Sobering up is painful, and when sober we think about what a mess we're making of everything, and so we get wasted again. There came a time for me when booze alone wasn't enough, and I knew there were other ways of getting wasted. I was never a massive fan of weed. Although I smoked a fair bit of it in my late teens I found it pretty boring. I preferred things that would make me lively rather than make me go to sleep. The first one I tried was magic mushrooms. I ate a couple of handfuls one morning when I was out in town with some college friends and waited to see what happened. After maybe half an hour I started to find everything amusing. Then everything started to look a little different to how it normally would. When the two things were combined I found myself laughing so much I could barely breathe. Someone showed me a cup of water and it seemed like the most ridiculous thing ever. Then someone turned up eating a cupcake with a serious expression on his face. This sent me into hysterics. That first trip I felt totally in control of even though I couldn't control the laughter. I just had a fabulous time, and I told someone that day that I wished I was tripping the whole time. "Don't do that, it's not a good habit to get into" she said, but I didn't see how anything could be bad when it made me so happy.

The effects had worn off after around four hours, and I couldn't wait to have some more, but at this point I still found it pretty hard to get hold of anything and so I had to wait. My next favourite became speed. The first time I had some I felt like I was living on fast forward but the world was still on the same pace. I was still high when I got home from a gig I'd been to, and I had a shower and washed my hair at great velocity. I listened to three Manic Street Preachers albums in a row from start to finish, just digesting every note and lyric, and then I listened to the first one again. The light was off in my room and towards the end I was seeing a miniature polar bear dancing in front of the stereo. I was desperate to feel that high again, and this time I didn't have to wait long. Over the following months I took it whenever I could get my hands on it, which wasn't infrequently, and I soon discovered how nasty a speed comedown could be. I remember at a party when I'd gone through a bag of the stuff the previous day I was starting to come down the next morning and was playing a Playstation game with some friends. One of them kept saying how bad I was at the game and all of a sudden I was back in the playground being taunted by the bullies. A comedown is like a hangover, but for me there was always a real psychological element, with emotions being heightened to crazy levels. In that moment I couldn't keep a lid on my sadness and had to go into another room, where I sobbed for a good few minutes. This wasn't uncommon on my comedowns, and probably wasn't helped by the fact that speed supresses your appetite and makes sleep fairly impossible to come by. Without these basic biological needs being met it's no wonder my emotions went haywire. I was drinking a fair bit too, and the combination can't have been doing my health any good.

Unfortunately for me I was hanging round with a number of people who had no interest in me stopping, because they were all on it too. I didn't make friends with people who were into healthy pursuits, because I didn't have much in common with them at that time and besides, I had an image to uphold. I was Dangerous Dave. I got wasted. That's just the way it was. That's what everyone knew me for, and if I stopped getting wasted then no-one would be interested in knowing me. Surely.

Around this time I found myself another girlfriend. She liked everyone to think she was depressed, and enjoyed drinking nearly as much as I did. She had incredibly low self-esteem and made herself feel better by feeling wanted. She was in a relationship when I met her, but that didn't stop her from asking if she could sit on my lap within about an hour of meeting me and then kissing me. I let her, and I kissed her back again and again. It didn't bother me that she had a boyfriend. In my drunken state I reasoned that if she cared about him then she wouldn't have kissed me, and besides I wanted to feel good about myself too. I didn't think I was worth anything, and was really lacking in empathy at this point so I just didn't care how it might effect this guy she was already with. What I didn't think much about at the time was that if she'd been willing to cheat on him so easily she would probably have eyes for others beside me too. She did. It broke my heart. I suppose I could say I got what I deserved because I'd known she had a boyfriend when she was introduced to me, but at a party we were at she pretty much slept with the guy who was meant to be my best friend at the time while I was in the next room. I was distraught, because I thought I was in love with her. I thought we were two broken people and that somehow we could mend each other, but instead we just seemed to bring out the worst in each other. I didn't carry on seeing her after that, and my supposed friendship with that guy never really recovered. I didn't eat much around this time. I wouldn't say I ever had an eating disorder, but was probably borderline here and there. It didn't seem like much of a problem though, because I seemed to be surviving. I saw eating as just something that needed to be done, a chore, and didn't really take any pleasure in it.

For a while I hit the booze and drugs harder than ever; I didn't know what else to do. A friend had the house to himself for a few weeks and so he invited a load of us round to get wasted for as long as we wanted. Today the idea of sitting in someone's house being off my face, surrounded by people who are off their faces, seems like such a waste of life but at the time it felt like I'd never been so alive. I felt like a rock star, and like I was part of the coolest party ever. Getting wasted took me to places that felt happy and comfortable, where my inhibitions and demons melted away and where I could hide from myself. Life was very much about the present, which is how it should be, but that was the only thing that was right about it. I remember one morning at that party wandering outside to some swings at the local park with a guy who I didn't know that well and having what felt like the most profound conversation ever. I don't remember what we talked about but pretty much anything seemed profound when we'd been up all night getting high. Many ultra runners speak of the incredible lift that comes when you've been running all night, starting to feel exhausted and demotivated, and then see the sunrise. It's perhaps something about the feeling of light at the end of the tunnel, or a ray of hope amid the darkness, but there's something about the sunrise that seems to stir up something in even the most cynical mind, which is what I had at this time for sure. Having said that, the sunrise also often meant the party would soon be over, which I didn't like. If I was lucky I could sleep off some of the disappointment and then get on it again.

If you're in a bad way sometimes you can be lucky enough to get a wake-up call. One of mine came at Glastonbury Festival in 1999. I once shared the observation with someone that at Glastonbury no matter how obliterated you are you can always console yourself with the fact that somewhere on the festival site someone will be lying in a ditch tripping their face off and thinking they're the gateway to a parallel dimension, and so there will always be someone in a worse state than you. However, on the Thursday night of that festival I'm not sure there were too many people in a worse state than I was.

I'd gone to the festival with my friends Gareth and Nick, and was excited that Gareth was up for doing some acid. He'd taken it a number of times before and I told him that I had too, reasoning that it must be pretty much like mushrooms and I could blag it, so we searched high and low for some all day on Thursday. No luck, and by the evening Gareth fancied a nap so Nick and me headed out for a stroll round the site. We walked up to the stone circle, and it wasn't long before a guy in a hoodie that was probably made somewhere in South America was stumbling towards us saying "Trips for sale." He took about thirty seconds to answer each of my questions, indicating that his was good stuff, and so we bought three tabs; one each. When we got back to the tent Gareth was annoyed at being woken up but when I said we had acid he leapt out of his sleeping bag. Our subsequent conversation went a little something like this: -

"We've got three."

"Why did you only get three?"

"They're red dragons. They're pretty strong."

"Why did you only get three?"

Nick didn't take one straight away. Gareth and me swallowed one each, and we all started to have a wander. For a couple of hours very little happened, and when Gareth suggested getting some more I couldn't think of any reason to disagree. We got some blank tabs off a guy who looked like a scientist, albeit a scientist who'd taken off the goggles, hung up his lab coat, put away the test tubes, switched off the Bunsen burner and decided to let his hair down, and we ate one each.

"You can definitely taste the acid" I said, not really knowing what it was meant to taste like.

"Like flip you can," snarled Gareth, "We've been stitched up."

That tab definitely had tasted of something to me but Gareth was the expert and so I thought I must be mistaken. We'd got two each and he said we may as well drop the other ones just in case there was anything on them at all. We did, and we swallowed half of Nick's each as well, which he offered us instead of paying towards a block of hash we'd bought. What happened next I recounted in a session with my second counsellor, Hannah, years later. It left me feeling pretty peculiar, and I can feel myself getting uneasy as I begin to write about it now, but I have to tell this story because it was when the old cliché about playing with fire and getting burnt hit home for the first time.

Basically around five minutes after we'd dropped the rest of the tabs the first ones began to properly take effect. I felt kind of like I had on mushrooms but straight away I felt less in control. We were chatting to some guys we'd met and I became suddenly aware of really needing a wee. I asked if there was a toilet nearby and one of the guys said there was a hedge just across the field.

"Where's the hedge?" I slurred.

"You really are fudged, aren't you?" laughed Gareth.

I managed to find the hedge but then going for a wee was the strangest experience I'd ever had. The stream of urine seemed to flow like water from a fountain, but then twisted and cascaded onto the ground, droplets scattering around the floor in different patterns. It seemed to go on for about ten minutes, but then when I looked at my watch I realised less than a minute had passed. When I started to walk back Gareth was there talking to a girl. She looked at me and I saw her as a wood nymph. I laughed and reached out to touch her arm, and she seemed to say "Neep" in a high pitched voice without opening her mouth and then the world revolved around her, literally not metaphorically, and I imagined her as a womble in human form. I'd heard that the effects of acid lasted for about eight hours. I was in for a long night.

I was kind of enjoying myself at this point but everything felt a little intense and so I suggested to Gareth we went and found somewhere to sit. Nick had wandered off back to the tent by this point, and so we went and joined some people sat round a small campfire. One of them was playing a didgeridoo and perhaps I can best describe his appearance by saying we referred to him all night as 'Gnome Shaman.' I looked into the flames and could see that instead of using firewood they appeared to be burning Mr Kipling cakes. Many hours passed by that fire and I tried to make conversation with the people sitting around but nothing seemed to make sense. I couldn't believe anyone could feel as out of touch with reality as I did and then ever feel normal again, so I guessed that no-one ever remembered how acid truly felt.

"It's probably like this every time" I kept saying, and of course in my head it made sense but no-one else knew what I was talking about. I also kept having to do reality checks. I tried to remember that my name was David James Urwin and I lived in Broadway, Somerset. If I could just remember those two things then it felt like everything would be Ok, perhaps because I'd heard these were the first two questions paramedics would ask people who'd woken up after being unconscious. I kept saying "This is my pocket. We're tripping at Glastonbury. That's Gareth's phone" and trying whatever I could to maintain a vague sense of what was going on. However, when a girl came and sat by the fire and told us that she'd just woken up I couldn't make sense of it. It wasn't morning. Surely everyone had been awake for hours. She said she had a hangover, but how could she? How much time had passed? Was it the next day? It seemed to be about two in the morning. At this point I'd been trying to light a cigarette for about twenty minutes, but performing the most simple task on acid can take forever. The best way I can describe it is like being a tiny child again, being asked to put your shoes on and then being distracted by a piece of lego on the floor, or seeing something out of the window, or suddenly realising you're hungry. Another way could be like being on facebook when you're trying to get something done. You're just about to put a stamp on that envelope but then a notification pops up and you forget all about the envelope, or the stamp, and then somebody sends you a message, and then you see somebody has posted some photos from their holiday. Half an hour passes and you are still no closer to being able to post that letter. There are distractions everywhere.

The hangover girl wanted to borrow my lighter and it had taken me so long to light my cigarette already that I just couldn't allow any further delays, but I couldn't articulate this to her and so I just kept scuttling away from her and laughing. I don't know how long it took to get my cigarette lit, but eventually I did, and then it seemed to be gone in about two puffs so I decided to have another. Of course the second and third trips kicked in on top of the first, and Gareth admitted he'd been wrong and we had actually dropped some quite potent acid. There was a point where all I could do was just lie there and try and make some kind of sense of what was going on around me. People were drumming everywhere, and I saw Scottish clansmen like those in the film Braveheart walking around with swords, preparing for battle. I wasn't scared, but I didn't know what I was feeling. Just after dawn a firework went off in the sky and I saw hundreds of tiny explosions as if I was looking through a kaleidoscope. I remember deciding to go for a walk at one point and I had my arms out like I was pretending to be an aeroplane. I tried to talk to a few people but they were all kind of weirded out by me, so in the end I just made my way back to Gareth. He suggested we went back to our tent because the trip would start to wear off soon, but I wasn't sure if he was right.

We commenced the journey back to the tent with Gnome Shaman as our guide, who didn't know where our tent was but considering how wasted Gareth and me were, he probably stood as much chance of finding it as we did. On the way back Gareth told me to buy a pack of cigarettes from a stall. I didn't think this was a bad idea but I looked at the guy behind the counter and his face was pulsating, so I wasn't entirely sure if I trusted him.

"Fags, twenty of them" I blurted out, relieved that I'd managed to form some kind of vaguely coherent sentence.

"I've only got packs of ten" he replied. My heart sank. I stared at him blankly for a little while and watched one of the hairs on his head fall off and then move in circles around his face. I briefly considered telling him about this, but I wasn't sure if I'd want to know if it had happened to me.

"Do you want a pack of ten?" he said.

"Er....yeah, sure" I muttered.

My next problem came when I had to remember how to carry out a transaction. I knew that I had to give him money, but did I have any? I then remembered about a thing called a wallet, and was a little perturbed when I felt that mine seemed to have turned into a frog in my pocket, but I took it out nonetheless, and luckily it became wallet shaped again when it was in my hand. I opened the zip and gazed at the notes, eventually settling on a twenty. If this had been happening in an actual shop outside of the festival the shopkeeper would probably have asked me to leave by now, but I guess he'd probably been used to this kind of thing throughout the night. I handed him the money and took the cigarettes, walking off towards Gareth. Luckily the guy on the stall was honest and called me back to give me my change. I could have done without the hassle, and I nearly just walked off without taking it but I went back and then took it from him, dropping it all over the floor and then searching around for the coins. Eventually satisfied that I had something like the right amount of money I gave Gareth one of the cigarettes and lit one myself, walking after him and Gnome Shaman. Every few steps they suddenly seemed to be about twenty metres in front of me and I kept having to call them back, but they were probably actually only a few steps away. All night I'd had a kind of metallic taste in my mouth, and it was starting to intensify. I also became aware that my teeth were a little sore from where I'd been gnashing them all night. The guys had to get me moving again a couple of times after I'd stopped to amuse myself by swooshing my cigarette through the air, because every time I'd done so it had made a trail. Hours of fun could have been had, but I use the word fun loosely. I knew I wasn't really enjoying myself, and just wanted to feel normal again.

To this day I have literally no idea how he managed it, but Gnome Shaman led us back to our tent, where an incredibly groggy looking Nick woke up and put his head out of the door. We laughed at him, and then checking what the time was I estimated that the trip may last a couple of hours yet.

"Great" moaned Nick, and we all laughed again.

Gnome Shaman soon left, and Gareth and me sat there smoking our cigarettes and eating hula hoops. We also had a can of John Smith's each, and at one point I can't remember what I said but

I'd made some kind of comment when Gareth had taken a sip of his beer. He stared me straight in the eye and smirked.

"You're still tripping your face off, aren't you?"

"Yes."

At this point I was a little worried. I wasn't sure if it was ever going to stop. When I'd taken mushrooms the first time I was disappointed when it was ending, but now I would have given anything for it to be over. Gareth had a nap. I hadn't wanted to go to sleep because I had an idea that I should stop tripping first and so I had a little wander. When I headed over to the portaloos I felt like everyone was looking at me and knowing what a state I was in. I walked a bit further and by every tent there was a Gareth and a Nick. Even if the people looked nothing like Gareth and Nick there was just something about them that made them the same. When Gareth woke up we walked to the Pyramid Stage to see the first band of the day, but I didn't want to stay there, so I walked all the way back to the tent.

The third scenario I described in the introduction is what happened when I got back there. I was scared. I wasn't in control, and all those months of getting wasted, not looking after myself and forgetting who I was were finally catching up with me. I was sat in that tent looking at myself in the mirror and realising that I just wasn't enjoying myself. I was terrified. I didn't know if I'd ever feel like myself again. After looking outside and seeing a cloud in the sky spinning round like a Catherine wheel I decided the only thing for it was to try and get some sleep. It took me a while to drop off, but I must have done because the next thing I remember is Gareth appearing in the tent doorway and me feeling back to normal again.

When I say back to normal I mean I wasn't tripping my face off any more, but that experience definitely left a mark on me. For the rest of that weekend I wasn't quite myself, and then for weeks after I got back I was trying to recount the experience to people but not really being able to explain it. I wouldn't touch any drugs for a long time after that, but it didn't stop me boozing. Thing is, because that was legal, or because I was nearly old enough to do it legally, it didn't seem so bad. The truth now is I believe that alcohol can be just as damaging as any illegal drug, but compared to acid it just seemed like a bit of harmless fun. Everyone did it. A little while after Glastonbury Festival I started to get a new lease of life, through going to a point where I thought I had lost my mind and then coming back from the edge. For a while I started to feel pretty contented within myself, and started listening to upbeat music like Terrorvision, Green Day and Reef. I got a new girlfriend, and my best friend at the time started going out with her neighbour, and I got into college again to study English Language, Philosophy and Biology (which I would soon change to Media Studies.) Even though I was still boozing as hard as ever a lot of the time I was living something approaching a normal life, and after my experiences at Glastonbury that was all I wanted. I just wanted normality and good, harmless fun. For a while that's exactly what I had.

Thames Trot 50 Miler
(5th February 2012)

Some time around October 2011 I signed up for the Thames Trot 50 miler, which would take place on 5th February 2012. I'd never run 50 miles before and so I researched how other people trained to do it. It seemed like the common answer was to run. A lot. I printed off a 50 mile training plan and decided to try and stick to it as much as I could, and so I started as soon as possible. I ran the training miles slowly, trying to stick to around 9-and-a-bit minute miles, because this is what I planned on running during the race, at least for the first half. Around New Year I had my usual winter depression and just wanted to get away from my usual surroundings for a while, so I set off for Oxford and decided to run the course in stages. I was glad I'd done this, because there were a couple of places it seemed like it would be easy to go wrong if you didn't know where you were going, and I got used to the kind of terrain I'd be up against. It was basically flat canal paths, a little muddy in places, with the odd bit of tarmac thrown in and then a couple of hills around 30 miles in.

I'd only known it was possible for a human being to run 50 miles for about a year, and now I was about to attempt it. Months of preparation, so how could I have slept through my alarm and my wake-up call? It was 7.45, the race was starting in an hour and I wasn't going to have time for breakfast or anything. Of course this was a dream, and I woke up with plenty of time to spare. I managed to polish off a bowl of bran flakes with some grapes, a slice of toast and jam and some orange juice for breakfast. There were a number of other runners sitting at tables in the hotel breakfast room, and I exchanged nods with them all. Talk of 100 milers made me think I was a little under-prepared, but as ever that didn't matter. I ran because I could, and I appreciated what others had achieved but I didn't let it make me feel inferior, because we were all in this together and we all had our individual goals. I was never going to be someone who won races, and found this extremely liberating.

At the start line, unknown to me at the time, some excellent British ultra runners lined up, including Robbie Britton, Dave Ross, Craig Holgate and Martin Bacon. I recognised Paul Stout and Paul Ali because they were dressed as Batman and Robin. As if these ultras weren't tough enough already. Unfortunately one of the portaloos at the start wouldn't flush, and so resembled one of the khazis from Glastonbury festival in the late 90s. I joked to the next bloke in line that I hoped it wasn't an omen for how my race was going to go. A few people said I was mental for wearing shorts. It was -7 degrees at the start by all accounts, and it certainly did feel a bit cold, but my Geordie blood would take care of that I hoped. Having said that it was pretty silly not to bring any gloves, and my hands felt freezing. What I was more worried about though to be honest was the prospect of trying to cover 50 miles on foot in under 11 hours. I knew I could run a marathon in training now in not much over 4 hours without really pushing it, but to run almost another one straight afterwards? Well, it was all about to become very real, as we were off.

We turned left out of the Prince of Wales pub car park and within a minute about 30 people in front of me ground to a halt. It quickly became clear why, as there was a huge patch of ice on the left-hand side of the road. Glad to avoid that one. I had planned on running 9.30-ish minute miles for the first hour, but negotiating a narrow bridge early on and being held up by all the people making their way through made this tricky straight away, and meant that once we got onto the path proper I had to run a little faster than I'd been hoping to so early on in order to get back on track. It felt Ok though, and a few conversations with other runners helped the early miles to pass quickly. About three miles in a guy's race number was flapping on his backpack and making a percussive noise that made it easy to keep a good rhythm. I commented on this to an Australian guy I was running alongside, and he agreed "Yeah mate, I'm definitely running to 113."

Batman blasted past a few miles in, to which I commented "Oh no, I can't be hallucinating already, surely?" and he replied "Nah, and it's not New Year's Eve either." I guess he'd heard that one before. Even though the frosty conditions made the ground hard, which became jarring before too long, there's something about running alongside a meandering river on a crisp February morning that makes it seem easier. A handful of dates after six miles also helped, and soon after that I remembered that blimey, I'm actually doing the Thames Trot now. I laughed to myself in the same way I remember doing during my European travels upon suddenly remembering "I'm in Romania!" or "I'm in Liechtenstein!" As we passed through the edge of Abingdon a number of people shouted their support from bridges, or the side of the path, and when we got to the first checkpoint at around mile 9.5 I was feeling great still. I only stopped for long enough to grab a few jelly babies. I hadn't needed to drink much water yet, so had plenty to be going on with.

On the way to checkpoint two I settled into a groove behind a guy in a luminous jacket, and decided to stay at his pace. This remained for around four miles before I decided as I was feeling so good I may as well get a few more miles in the bank, and so I accelerated just a little. This led to me meeting Gordon from Ireland, who had not run for four weeks due to a stress fracture. I remember thinking how hardcore he was, and was delighted to see later on that he'd finished in a little over 10 hours. The course meandered further along the river before emerging into Shillingford, where a road crossing had to be negotiated, and then another shortly afterwards. A fair bit of Saturday traffic meant this wasn't as easy as I wanted it to be, but I was still able to keep up a reasonable pace at this point, and came into the second checkpoint still feeling strong. I decided to sample some of the famous fruit cake that had been talked up before the race, and got them to mix me some sports drink. I told my parents that I was still feeling good and set off sharpish.

The next section involved a diversion due to work being carried out on a bridge, and so we followed the roads to Wallingford. On the way, after discovering that the fruit cake was delicious and that the sports drink tasted of Paracetamol, my dad drove past sounding his horn. I was pleased that I was still able to run well at this stage. However, it was after getting back on the path out of Wallingford that I first started to feel a downturn. I think it was partly due to this section being muddy, and a lot of mud gathering on the bottom of my shoes, adding weight to my feet. Also due to having run 22 miles barely pausing for breath, and thinking about how far there was still to go. As I would discover, so much of ultra running is psychological. Not long after this I stopped for a wee by a tree and was pleased to see that it was a good colour, as pure as a mountain stream, so my hydration seemed to be spot on. I pressed on, and soon a couple of guys who I passed going through a small wooded area told me that I was moving well. I wasn't sure I agreed, but if they thought so then I'd take it as the boost I needed.

The next couple of miles seemed to drag on forever. I was beginning to feel quite fatigued at this point, and had to run/walk over the fields past huge flocks of geese, who I feared may think I was encroaching on their territory and would want to chase me. They didn't, and I managed to run reasonably strongly into the third checkpoint. I had read that this one would be well stocked with savouries, and so had planned to stop here for a few minutes and have something to eat, but there was little for vegetarians. My dad handed me a few chips but they didn't seem too appetising, and I tried to put down some more water. My parents were asking me questions but I wasn't able to answer in full sentences. This was around 28.5 miles in, and I must admit at this stage I first started to have real doubts as to whether I'd make it. My mum looked worried and so I gave her a hug before I left. I'd also made a poorly judged comment, saying there were some hills coming up soon, in front of a guy who looked like the idea of walking another mile on the flat wasn't too appealing. I told him they weren't too big, which was kind of true, although they would seem it with 30 miles in our legs.

So, onward bearded warrior. No sooner had I crossed the nearby bridge then I retched a few times. I'd read that top ultra runners consume around 300 calories per hour during races, and didn't know how this was possible. I guess it's about training your body to cope, but my nauseous feelings stopped me from keeping a good pace going for a little while. At mile 30 a few local teenagers sprinted past me saying "Keep it going, keep it going, come on!" I felt like making a sarcastic comment about it being easy for them to say, but then one of them gave me a sweet and I remembered they were only trying to help. Then we hit the hills. I remember little about them, except that it was a massive psychological battle to keep moving forwards, or upwards I guess I should say, and that I made a few groaning sounds at the injustice of it all. Then when we finally got to the top we had to go down again, which was tough on the quads at this stage. Ouch.

Eventually I got to the checkpoint at Mapledurham, 35 miles in, and said to my parents "I feel bloomin' horrible, but I'll keep going." My dad gave me a can of coke, which I was very grateful for, and I took a piece of cake with me for the trudge up the last real hill on the course. I couldn't manage more than a bite or two, but the coke gave me a real lift. It was a can of coke, remember. I chatted a bit with a guy during the climb who'd done the Thames Trot three times, and said he found it really challenging still. He thought it was partly the relentless nature of the flat course making it hard on the legs. Ironic that he was telling me this during one of the few hill climbs. Reaching the top of the hill there was another very short climb, and then a descent down a massive flight of steps. As soon as I reached the bottom of these something lifted, and a huge sense of calm washed over me. I was able to get into a fairly decent (for this late in the race anyway) running pace again at last.

I did a lot of thinking on this section, mostly about how much of ultra running is down to psychology. Before I'd run a marathon anything beyond that seemed preposterously far, but then there was a time when the same was true of a half-marathon, or a 10k, or a 5k. The reason it seemed preposterous was because I didn't know what it was like to go further. The unknown is often what makes things seem preposterous. Everything I'd read about ultras was coming true. I had hit low points, but I'd just tried to keep moving forward in any way I could, had fuelled as much as possible, and then I broke through them. As I was running past the outskirts of Reading on the path next to the river I had covered over 40 miles on foot, but I still had running left in me. Myself and two South African guys kept passing each other along this stretch, and always had a few words of encouragement for each other. Similarly with an older guy, and his even older pacer, who had just come out to run with his friend for a couple of miles. I've always felt a huge sense of camaraderie with ultras. Everyone I passed, or who passed me in the latter stages, paused to chat for a little while. As I reached the final checkpoint at Sonning, with just over 5 miles to go, I high-fived everyone and as the guy at the checkpoint read my race number 94 I said "Incidentally, I feel like I am about 94 right now." One of the South African guys said "You don't look a day over 30." I asked him how he knew I was 30 and he said it was because of my legs. I scoffed a few more jelly babies and some twiglet type snacks, then it was time for the final push. With almost 3 hours to go before the cut-off I knew I was going to make it, although I did say nothing was guaranteed when my legs were feeling as bad they were. I have to say I can't remember how bad my legs did feel at this stage. The mind has a way of forgetting how much it hurt afterwards. If it didn't I doubt many people would put themselves through it again.

Anyway, it was starting to get very gloomy by now, and a light dusting of snow was beginning to fall. I was able to run much of the final stage, but only at around 10 minute miles. I must say a couple of times I stopped to walk simply to savour the moment. The coating of snow that was beginning to form on the fields in the twilight was just so beautiful, especially with the endorphin high that comes from running so far. As I reached the village of Shiplake the snow was lit up by the old-fashioned street lamps that you see many of in Oxfordshire, and I began to laugh out loud to myself. About twenty months prior to this I'd been utterly euphoric to run my first 10k, and after that I'd not run much until about March the next year. Now here I was about to complete a 50 mile ultra. I had to shout out to two guys that were taking a wrong turn and they were very grateful. Extra miles at that stage would hurt. As we got out of the village and into what I knew was the last field before the finish at Henley-on-Thames I decided to walk once more and gathered myself for the final run into the finish. Tempered with the euphoria of being so close to the finish was a feeling that I didn't want this to end just yet. After all, when would I get to feel like this again?

I got to the end of the field and began to run along the bridges that take you to the final stretch. The thin layer of snow lit up by the fairy lights along the bridge made this pretty magical, and I don't think I'll ever forget that image. I continued to run alongside the river, and could see the lights that must have been where the finish was. People applauded and said "Well done" as I passed, and I tried hard not to be overwhelmed. One of the last people said the finish was about 200 yards up on the left. Very soon after this, as the snow got heavier, the finish line came into view. As soon as I saw it I exploded with euphoria and began to sprint for the line. This really seemed to stir up the spectators who lined the way, and as I crossed the line I threw my hands in the air and bellowed at the top of my voice. Overwhelmed was not the word. This had been like life in a day. There were huge low points but I got through them, and in the latter stages I began to realise that everything was going to be Ok as long as I kept believing.

I'd finished in just over 9 hours. However, whether it had been just under 11 hours, 7 hours or anything in between that just wasn't important. What mattered was that I'd overcome adversity, and if I could do that in an ultra then maybe I could do it in life too. On the way home we stopped at a service station for some horrible food, my body was craving it, and the moment I got out of the car I shouted in pain and could only hobble to the building, but at the same time I was laughing. Yet another thing I was reminded of was that pain is temporary. When I woke up the next morning my legs were shouting at me "Why, Dave? WHY?!!!" and walking up or down stairs took forever, but I didn't care. For the next few days I rested, ate everything in sight and basked in the glory of achieving something that had seemed completely impossible not long ago. I said to my mum the morning after the race that I reckoned if it had been 62 miles (100k) I could have finished. If it had been 100 miles I wasn't so sure, but ultras really are just a matter of faith. As long as you look after yourself during the race and are lucky enough not to get injured it really comes down to just how much you want to finish. If you want it enough you will find a way.

False Confidence

Long, long ago in the time before the digital age my uncle Chris climbed right to the top of the bridge over the river Wear in Sunderland and sat there playing a mouth organ before climbing down again. Had he done this yesterday it's entirely possible that by now there would be a video clip of it on Youtube, and within minutes the police would have arrived to arrest him, or perhaps try and talk him down, thinking he was going to jump. This is one of the main differences between life then and now. Back then events were special, because 99 times out of 100 you actually had to be there to see them. There's no way of knowing how many people saw it, although there is a video on Youtube of a young Russian woman climbing to the top of a radio tower with her boyfriend and playing a flute. Is it possible that her uncle, or grandfather, had been a Russian sailor who had been on a boat passing through at the time and told stories upon his return home of 'that crazy Englishman', which were passed down to the next generation?

The two things are probably entirely unconnected, but the reason I told this story is that Chris has said he doesn't know to this day how he managed the climb. I think I can explain. He was drunk. There are a couple of key elements in being able to do something. The first is wanting to, and the second is believing you can. After that it's usually within the realms of possibility. Chris wasn't a particularly seasoned climber, but the alcohol would have removed the inhibitions that would normally have prevented him from attempting to get to the top of that bridge. I've come to this conclusion because alcohol always made me fearless. Without it I was a shy, retiring person. With it I was a nightmare. After my experience at Glastonbury 1999 I eased off for a while, and as a result I felt myself slowly retreating into my shell. People remarked that I'd become quieter and didn't seem quite as crazy as before. For a while I was happy about that, as it seemed that the opposite had nearly made me lose touch with reality forever, but it wasn't too long before I started to miss the person I was when I was wasted. I missed the lack of inhibitions more than anything.

By late 2000 I was back to being Dangerous Dave again, and when I was wasted I found it easy to stay in character. Sometimes even when I wasn't. I can recall once or twice telling stories to a captive audience of people who were crowding around me, keen to hear my latest tales of debauchery. I loved the attention. When I'd grown up being so unpopular it felt amazing to be considered an interesting character, even if it was for reasons I knew were the wrong ones deep down. Therefore I knew I had to keep up the image, and so every weekend I would get absolutely annihilated. People seemed to think it was awesome, and so I believed them. I knew it was taking its toll on my health though. One day during summer 2001 just the scent of the kebab meat from outside a shop was enough to send my empty stomach into turmoil and I was violently sick. I was also deeply unhappy, and it's no wonder when I was so unhealthy. I don't think I ever ate any fruit or vegetables on purpose around this time, even though I was a vegetarian, and I would sometimes go a couple of days without sleep, which of course didn't help.

I stumbled my way through college and somehow got into Bath Spa University College to study Creative Writing. Not because I particularly wanted to, but because I thought it was the best chance I had of winning at life. My first night at Uni set the tone for most of my time there. I drank way too much on a near empty stomach, behaved strangely, offended a few people and then spent much of the next week in my room listening to music, smoking and feeling depressed. I'd hit the booze and drugs hard that summer, and had once again thought I'd fallen in love with a girl. She didn't love me back, and as a result I thought life was hideously unfair and was better spent intoxicated. Looking back now I was pretty close to having psychosis once or twice, and I became withdrawn and paranoid. Also I was always the guy at the party who would stay up when everyone else had gone to bed getting wasted on his own. I didn't want to go to bed, because then I knew when I woke up I'd be sober. I wanted the intoxication to go on for as long as it possibly could, and was pretty unimpressed when people didn't share my enthusiasm. "This town's full of wetties" I once said to a room full of the kind of people my mum always warned me about as a young child. I didn't mean them, but they could easily have thought I did.

I didn't really go to many lectures in the first year, just like my first year at college, but somehow I did just enough to scrape through. I was living in halls and as I got to know my housemates better I became pretty good friends with them. Two of them, Ross and Emma, got together during Fresher's Week and are now married with a child. There were definitely some fun times, the trouble is I'm struggling to remember many of them because pretty much most of that first year I was either drunk or depressed, or both. I was terrible with money, most of my student loan going on booze and vinyl records in the first few weeks, and throughout the rest of the year I had to keep extending my overdraft and applying for hardship funds/loans. Sometimes I had literally no money and lived on a couple of big plates of pasta a day, being thoroughly miserable because I had no money for booze. If I was lucky sometimes someone would lend me enough for a bottle of vodka.

The times I felt most confident at Uni were when I was drunk, but doubly so when my mates from home came to visit. At this time there were a group of six of us; me, Bob, Sergio, Tris, Chuffy and Jay, and although we were only ever all together in one place about once we were best friends, and having people who knew me well, had seen the worst of me and still wanted to know me meant I felt invincible when they were around me. There was usually a bit of havoc when my friends came to visit. My favourite story is when Sergio was staying for a weekend and we managed to cover four walls with a drunken stir-fry we made and then ate four yoghurts that we thought belonged to my housemate Rachel, who was away for the weekend. We were going to replace them the next day and she would never know. We went upstairs and passed out.

We came downstairs in the morning with the worst hangovers that anyone's ever had, ever.

"We're going into town," I groaned, "Does anyone want anything?"

"Oh, could you get me some yoghurts please?" said my housemate Hannah.

"Sure, what kind?"
"Oh I don't know, maybe the ones you ate!"

Oops. Her expression persuaded me it wasn't a good idea to say any more, just to go and replace the yoghurts. She had been poorly that weekend and had woken up in the night wanting something to eat. A yoghurt was the only thing she'd felt she could manage, but they were all gone. It turned out Ok, because not only did we replace them with twice as many but we bought her a bunch of flowers, snowdrops, which happened to be her favourites. That was pretty lucky because they'd been the cheapest ones on the stall.

In the summer term I didn't often have money to drink and so I spent most of my time reading books in bed. I had dreadful insomnia most of the time when I couldn't drink, and I would often end up doing everyone's dishes during the night time, which I found quite therapeutic. Sometimes I would walk the couple of miles into town from the halls, which were at the out of town campus, at seven in the morning when I'd been up all night. I couldn't afford to get the bus back, so I'd walk back again, and if I was lucky I'd be able to grab a few hours' sleep. I was also trying to write a novel at this time. I'd never heard of Marcel Proust's 'In Search of Lost Time' at this point, but I guess it's what I was trying to write my own version of. I'd kind of given up on my own life, and so was trying to write something instead. My main character was called Fred Bacon and he was an acid casualty who had a kind of best friend/carer named Derek. Most of the writing was lengthy monologues from Fred, in which his brain would go off on all kinds of tangents and he would describe in minute detail things like making a hand-rolled cigarette or eating some toast. My lecturer thought it had some potential, but I clearly didn't because I gave up on it after about four chapters.

In the summer of 2002 my friend John took his own life. I was at Chuffy's one evening watching a film and our mate Dave tried to call me. I didn't answer because the film was on, but then he called again almost straight away and so I thought it might be important. I answered, and the conversation went something like this: -

"Hello?"

"Hey mate, it's Dave."

"Hey, how are you?"

"I've been better."

"Really?"

"Yeah, I guess you haven't heard about John."

"No, what about him?"

"He's dead, mate. He hanged himself."

At first it just seemed totally surreal. John? Why would he kill himself? He was one of the most passionate, enthusiastic people I knew. He was a DJ, like me, and would talk my ear off about all the new tunes he'd got every time I saw him, and he was always smiling. I guess this was when I really should have learnt that you never know what's going on under the surface. If someone seems confident it can often be a front. I had a problem, because his funeral was scheduled for the next week, when I was meant to be going on holiday with my family. I wanted to be at the funeral, but if I did my family wouldn't be able to enjoy their holiday, because I couldn't afford to go unless I got a lift up with them. I went on the holiday, and drank for most of it. This did include a night at the local pub where Joe and me told our dad about some of the things we'd got up to, and he found it all pretty amusing. Was probably the first time we'd all gone drinking together. The next morning my dad popped in there and one of the locals was thoroughly impressed that I'd been drinking shots of this home brewed Aftershock style drink that I'd spied behind the bar. At least I was impressing people in some way.

I always felt guilty for not being at John's funeral, and when I got back I was at a couple of parties where people were talking about it. At one of them I lost it a little, and ended up shouting at Sergio for something really insignificant, before pouring water over a couple of strangers and I think challenging one of them to a fight, which I'd never really done to anyone in my life. They didn't fight me, either because they felt sorry for me or because I seemed a bit unhinged, but either way I was beginning to show signs of being unwell. The next morning I apologised to everyone, but it didn't stop me drinking again before long. When I got back to Uni it was pretty much all I did again, taking advantage of some special offers at the local off-license.

During late 2002 I began to write a sitcom with Sergio. It was going to be called 'Push my Badger' and was about a couple of guys named Spike and Kevo who shared a flat and got into all kinds of surreal situations. It was mostly based on real life events, albeit real life imagined events. Spike and Kevo were based on when we'd been asked to DJ at a local jubilee disco. We were going to behave ourselves mostly and play a load of 80s stuff, 90s indie classics etc. but we were going to finish with a happy hardcore tune named 'Shooting Star', imagining a couple of thirty-something ex-ravers shouting "YES!!!" and charging onto the dancefloor, leading to an unfortunate rekindling of their old ways.

"Remember this one, Spike?" one of them would say.

"Course I do, Kevo" The other would reply.

My favourite bit of the whole script was a short sketch in which two posh guys were standing side by side in an expensive looking house and one of them would say "I like what you've done with the curtains", then the camera would pan round to the curtains and they would be on fire. We also had a character named Chunk who got places before people, simply because one day we'd been going to get petrol and Sergio said "Can we go to that pump?.... Nah, Chunk's got there first!" when a gorilla of a man drove into the space before us, giving us a look that dared us to complain.

We hoped at the time that Push my Badger would allow us to make a TV sitcom and make a bit of money, basically allowing us to not have to get a proper job. It was nearly all we talked about for months, and when we posted the script off in January 2003 it felt like our lives were about to change. Mine certainly was, but not in the way I expected.

New Forest Marathon (23rd September 2012)

This one was meant to be a training run for Norfolk Coastal Ultra, a 100k I was to attempt in October 2013, but I had also never run a sub 4 hour marathon at this point and this was definitely my goal. I don't know if you've heard of Drymax socks, a special type of sock a number of ultra runners swear by that apparently keeps your feet dry and helps prevent blisters, but I don't own any. No, I'm all about Frymax. Frymax is a special type of oil that is used by some fish & chip shops and is apparently better for you than what most chip shops use. The day before my first serious attempt at a sub 4 marathon I went to Lyme Regis with Boldebort and we ate chips and ice-cream. The chip shop in Charmouth is the best either of us have ever been to, and they are one of the places that uses Frymax. Perhaps the two things are linked. Either way, I was hoping this unconventional approach to pre-race fuelling would not hamper my chances of running a good race. I drove up that night to Salisbury, where I stayed at the YHA hostel in a dorm room full of old men, who mercifully just wanted to sleep and none of whom came in steaming drunk at 3am, so I actually slept pretty well. I had bought some home made flapjack from the hostel for the morning, which I devoured on the drive to New Milton. It was obvious straight away that the weather forecast had not been lying and I was probably in for a little bit of a soaking. Never mind, at least I would be kept cool. To sum up my marathon experiences again to date, I had never really nailed one before. I'd only done one official marathon race, which was the fairly tough, mostly off-road Somerset Levels and Moors Marathon (SLAMM) on my 30th birthday, but I had done several marathon length training runs, so I wasn't a stranger to the distance. Mind you, my quickest one yet was about 4 hours, 10 minutes.

I didn't fancy my chances of going that much quicker, knowing as I did from a number of tales and from reading the race booklet that this course had some hills. Also, this was meant to be a training run for my next ultra. Basically I had no expectations, and as I arrived at the recreation area very early to find a handful of other runners in rainproof jackets, and with solemn expressions, I realised that this would be a day just to see what happens. Being someone prone to melancholy episodes, I always find events like these a time to just be in the present and be me and enjoy the experience, and so I bantered with the folk at the information tent and wandered the streets to see if any shops were open. I managed to find a banana and a can of lime juice from a newsagents, which were certainly better than nothing, and when I got back I bumped into Nadya, a runner who I'd spoken to a number of times on a running forum but had never met in person. We had a laugh about how shoddy the conditions were and then joined in the rather fun half-marathon warm-up. The half started a while before the marathon, and so I saw the start of that race and then began a second warm-up. Warm-up is an ironic term by the way, because it has to be said it was pretty Baltic out there. I was thinking though that this may work in my favour as I'm definitely not a heat runner, and with it being this cold I didn't think I'd want to stop and walk even if I was exhausted. The forecast was for high winds and heavy rain as the race progressed. I smiled to myself and wandered over to the starting area.

At the start I met a runner named Ben, who was going for a sub 4 hour finish. He was impressed by my ultra running tales and seemed to massively overestimate my running skills, as much as I tried to play them down. We ended up running the first 4 or 5 miles together as we chatted, and this made the miles fly by. However, I managed to keep to my planned 8.45ish minute miles early on. In previous marathons I'd made the grave mistake of upping the pace early on because I felt strong, which had come back to haunt me in the final miles. Ben did drop off my pace a little at around 5 miles but at this point I started to run with a lady whose name I never knew, who had run London marathon the year before and said it was the most horrible experience she'd ever had, yet here she was again on a tougher course. There's something about the marathon that keeps people coming back for more. Anyway, we moved on out into the stunning scenery of the New Forest proper. The course was certainly undulating at this stage but I found all of the hills very runnable, and as ever was getting into the spirit of things by whooping and busting out the odd dance move for the marshalls and spectators. I was well impressed with these people, who were standing around for ages in truly horrendous weather. Far more impressive than running a marathon in it.

At around mile 8 I realised that I was feeling pretty strong, and so I went with it and upped the pace just slightly, but still took care to stay above 8 minute miles at all times. It reminded me a little of that classic of world cinema 'Speed' from the 90s, which details the plight of the bus driver accidentally caught up in the evils that sadly carry on in the hearts of some men. Mind you, I didn't have a bomb tied to me, so it wasn't that much like the film. At different times I fell into pace with an individual or group, and then dropped them all one by one, despite keeping to a very manageable pace. We crossed one of the off-road sections and ran through numerous deep puddles, without Drymax socks (for me, can't speak for anyone else), but at no point did I worry about blisters. I was loving it. I took a gel from one of the checkpoint volunteers and made sure I stayed on top of my fluid intake, although at any time I could have just opened my mouth and taken care of that probably, such was the strength of the downpour.

I passed the half way mark in 1 hour, 51 minutes and was still feeling strong, waving my arms and cheering the spectators, one of whom stared in shock and said "I don't know how they do it." Well running in torrential rain may not be everyone's idea of fun but very little makes me feel so alive. At around mile 16 there was a small out and back section, at which I managed to see that Ben was only a few minutes behind me, and we exchanged shouts of

"Looking strong" and "Good work" as we crossed. I was waiting for the wall to hit, but three miles later it still hadn't. Mind you, at this point five New Forest Ponies decided it would be fun to join in the race. They would run alongside us and then suddenly stop, leaving us wondering if we were about to be trampled, but eventually they sauntered off in a different direction, and not having been maramlised by the local wildlife put an extra spring in my step. On I trotted.

As mile 20 came and went the wall still hadn't hit. I had another gel at this point, and a woman on a mission who had an orange club vest of some kind on stormed past me. I had to use every ounce of restraint not to get drawn into her race and to keep to the pace that felt right for me. At this point I felt sub 4 could be on, but I also knew that at some point my legs would probably go. The miles seemed to be going by a lot slower by this point, but those markers still came.....22......23....ooh blimey, who put that steep hill there? Yes, at around mile 23 was the nastiest climb of the whole race. However, the race organisers had put inspirational quotes on boards going up the hill. I can't remember many, but a few said 'Are your legs Kenyan?', 'Pain is temporary, pride is forever' and 'Runners of the New Forest Marathon have the best legs.' Well they provided a nice distraction, and helped the top of the climb arrive quicker. When I got to the top and realised I could still run I began to dare to dream.

With 2 miles to go my legs started to protest a little, but not to the extent where I slowed down all that much. I fell into pace with a guy who had also been aiming for a sub 4, and he was saying "You've got it now, mate. Me too, we've got this." I said I didn't want to speak to soon, but it was looking good at the moment. Those last 2 miles seemed to take quite a long time, and during the last mile my whole body was beginning to beg me to stop, but just one more effort and then I could rest. This I knew. The point came where I knew I could walk to the finish and still make it in under 4 hours, and so I thought I may as well give it my all. Finally the crowds of spectators came into view and I heard my name and club announced over the tannoy system. As I entered the finishing corridor I thought "This is it", but then the corridor stretched on....and on.....and on. The marathon distance came up on my watch and I still couldn't see the finish. "Where's the finish?" said the guy I'd been running with, and then finally it came into view. A surge of adrenaline shot through my legs and I staggered a little bit faster than I had been. A quick glance at the finishing clock, and a massive smile swept across my face. I screamed with joy as I crossed the line. A lady wrapped a silver foil blanket round my shoulders and I looked at my watch, barely believing what it said. 3 hours and 47 minutes.

So let me get this straight. I'd smashed 4 hours on a hilly course in atrocious weather conditions. Splendid! Ben crossed the line with a triumphant shout about seven minutes later, and after congratulating him I tried to get warm. A cup of sugary tea did the trick, and then somehow I managed to drive home and was buzzing for a few days afterwards. The next weekend I ran Bristol Half Marathon in a new personal best time of 1 hour, 37 minutes. I'd run the first 9 miles with my old friend Chazz, but then he'd pulled away and finished about 4 minutes before I did. He'd projectile vomited as soon as he crossed the finish line, so I didn't mind missing that. Our friend Dave, known as Acidic Dave at college, finished a little way behind us and then we all went for a roast at a pub, where I managed to break the card machine by taking my card out before it was ready. A lot of things kept breaking around me at that time. Dave had broken a railing in Chazz's bathroom after the race, and Chazz's girlfriend Nicole had put her phone in the washing machine. Not too long after that my trusty red Peugeot Fliskin had broken down, for good. Oh yeah, and I broke two personal bests in two weeks. Not a bad lead-up to my first attempt at 62 miles.

Breakdown

One Saturday in early February 2003 I set off for Reading to my housemate Hannah's birthday party. I had to wait until well into the afternoon to set off, because the night before I'd got absolutely trolleyed with Joe and a bunch of his friends at a local pub. I had known them something wasn't quite right, because just before I was about to go out I was in the bathroom putting some aftershave on and suddenly my heart started racing, just out of nowhere. This triggered a few memories, such as a few weeks earlier when I'd suddenly felt a little light-headed whilst sat at the downstairs computer, but then I'd shaken my head and it had passed. Something similar had happened on my 21st birthday the previous September, where I'd thought I had a cold when I woke up in the morning but then the feeling passed throughout the day.

At times like this I thought back to that night at Glastonbury festival in 1999. That wasn't the only time I'd lost control either. I'd been to Amsterdam with my mate Jay in early 2002 and we'd eaten some quite potent mushrooms. We sat on a bench for a while laughing until our stomachs hurt as the houses danced, then Jay said "It's really weird that I've got a family," meaning it didn't make sense to him in his tripped out state. I began to think about it, then I stood up and things went haywire. I started walking down the street and couldn't stop myself from walking at great speed, then I fell over. We went into our hostel and got into the lift. Jay looked concerned, which made me worse, and I could see my eyeball hundreds of times in the lift mirror, like a kaleidoscope, just like when the firework had exploded in the sky at Glastonbury. We got up to our room and I told Jay I'd have to try and sleep it off, but I thought maybe that was it this time. Maybe I'd stay like this forever. I closed my eyes and saw lots of colourful patterns, and thought 'Well if I'm stuck with this from now on I may as well try and enjoy it', so I just watched the pretty patterns and smiled. It was this letting go and not fighting it any more that enabled me to come back to myself slowly, and before long we were out getting something to eat. I was still tripping but it was under control. There were other times on both acid and mushrooms that I seemed to take a long time to come down, the problem was often that I'd been up all night as well and was confusing the normal mild hallucinatory experience of sleep deprivation with a failure to come down off the trip, or perhaps one just exacerbated the other, but either way I went close to the edge on a few occasions. I held the trauma of it with me I guess.

As I explained earlier, I think the root of my anxiety illness was perhaps when my ancestors saw William Penfound's murder. Perhaps the buried trauma of that still existed in my family, and with every bad trip, every experience I couldn't understand and with John's suicide and my feelings surrounding it that trauma was getting closer and closer to the surface.

I got to Reading and didn't really feel like drinking because I wasn't feeling all that well, but I couldn't relax without a drink that evening, so I had a few pints. Then I hit the tequilas, or aftershocks, or something. I can't really remember. My main memory of that night is being too drunk and telling all Hannah's friends how miserable I was, and how low my self-esteem was. Quite understandably they found me to be killing the vibe a little, and so I was left on my own. I kept drinking, until I was left face down at a table. I guess I got back to Hannah's mum's house somehow because I woke up in the spare room there the next morning feeling utterly worthless. I was sick of this life. Sick of making an idiot of myself. Sick of being miserable. Sick of not feeling like I had a future. I'd half forgotten about the fact that I might be contacted by the BBC any day now to say they wanted to take mine and Sergio's script forward. We'd not heard anything yet, and so I felt I had no hope to hold onto.

A couple of my housemates wanted a lift back to Bath. I hadn't been planning on going that way, but I said I would. On the drive back I didn't feel quite right. I can't explain how, but I just knew something was wrong. We went for a roast dinner in a pub for lunch and then went back to my house. I still had to drive back to my parents' house and they were going to give me a lift back up, because I couldn't afford to run the car in Bath. I'd had a strange pressure feeling in my head for a couple of hours and was completely exhausted. I didn't want to drive back, but I had to. At the end of the journey the second scenario described in the introduction took place. I thought at first I might be having a heart attack, but then the pins and needles subsided and I was able to get my breathing under control and get back in the car, driving the mile or two back home. When I got back I told my parents how I was feeling and they said I probably had a virus, which I agreed with. I didn't really want to go back to Bath that night but a new term was beginning and I didn't want to miss too much of it and fall further behind.

As soon as I was dropped off I knew something was really not right. I sat down in the living room and my housemate Anna was telling me about her weekend. She hadn't had the best time and was venting a little, and normally I would have been fine with it. We used to watch a lot of films together and would talk about many things, good and bad, but at that moment I just didn't want to listen. I was feeling on edge, and like something dreadful was about to happen to me, and as she was talking I was just thinking 'Shut up.' I quickly decided I would be safest up in my room, and so I made my excuses and headed up there. I put a new CD on, I think it was 'Spirit of Eden' by Talk Talk, and I just couldn't listen to it. I turned it off and said "That's depressing" out loud, and was making a horrified face, as if it had been a personal attack on me. I tried to read, but I couldn't concentrate even for a minute. What was wrong with me? I was awake pretty much all night just going out of my mind with worry. I thought in the morning I'd go and see the doctor, or ring my parents and get them to come and pick me up, or talk to my housemates or something. If I could just get through to the morning maybe I'd be Ok. I was actually a little worried I might die before that happened though. Incidentally, I'd had a letter from the BBC that day saying that they weren't going to be commissioning 'Push my Badger', and disappointing as that was, it was now the least of my worries.

I don't know how I got through that night, I don't really remember, but when the sun came up things didn't feel quite so harrowing. I can't remember if I went back to my parents' house that day or if it was a few days later, but I know I went back and forth a few times over the next few weeks. A couple of times whilst in Bath I went to hospital feeling like I couldn't breathe properly but felt better once I was there. It's obvious now I was having panic attacks, but at the time I had no idea what a panic attack was and didn't understand the concept that I might be someone who could have one. I didn't understand how I could feel as ill as I did if there wasn't something seriously wrong with me. The only time I felt Ok was when I was drunk, and so I did a lot of drinking. It helped me forget. At the end of the third week I got a lift back with my housemate Laura, whose parents lived a few miles from mine. I got her to drop me about a mile's walk from my house all the same, rather than take me to my front door. My mum worked with children with learning difficulties at the school across the road, so I had to go there to get a key as I didn't have mine. On the walk back I'd felt my energy draining further and further, and when I got to the school I really didn't want to go in, but I knew if I just made that one final effort I'd have the key and could go and try and relax in the house. I remember going into the building and one of the teachers asking me a question. I just kind of said "Er..." and looked a little awkward. At that moment the school secretary, who had worked there when I was a pupil, saved me by appearing and saying she had the key for me. I went home and walked in the front door, but being there didn't bring me any comfort.

I'd been to a couple of doctors and they'd said I must just have a virus and had told me to rest and drink plenty of water. I kept going back, so they gave me antibiotics. Nothing seemed to be working. I sat in the house and waited for my mum to get back from work. I didn't really know what I would say to her when she did get back, but I guess I was hoping, like I hoped of everyone else at the time, she might have some kind of magical solution.

I just didn't know what to do with myself. That evening I sat down to dinner but just couldn't face it, so I went upstairs, but I didn't know what to do when I got there. I couldn't read, listen to music, write, sit still or do anything for very long at all without starting to panic about how I was feeling and wondering what was wrong with me. My mum would ask me if I wanted to do a number of different things but I didn't really want to do anything. Well, I would have loved to have done something, anything that would have taken my mind off how I was feeling, but I couldn't focus on anything.

What followed was basically a whole summer spent mostly in my parents' house. Most of the time I was just frantically trying to work out what was wrong, and I couldn't find the answer. I had a chronic sinus infection at the time, which the doctors did find out, but I always knew there was more to it than that. A sinus infection doesn't give you panic attacks and make you feel like you're losing your mind. Being indoors all day no doubt made me worse, but I couldn't face going outside. A few times my parents tried to take me places but I couldn't leave the house without having a panic attack, and I got frustrated with myself for this and with them for trying to make me go out when I wasn't ready. They always had my best interests at heart, and it must have been a fairly impossible situation, but I knew I had to get better in my own time and it couldn't be forced. I had well-meaning friends inviting me out as well, and sometimes Sergio, Bob or Chuffy would come and visit me, but I just couldn't explain to them what was wrong, because I didn't know myself.

Sometimes I was able to do things to pass the time. I must have played a thousand games of Scrabble with my mum that summer, and sometimes I would do crosswords. Somehow I even managed to get my Uni work done and go in the car with my dad to Bath to hand it all in one day. Once or twice I even managed to venture out for an evening at Sergio's, which was only a couple of miles away, but most of the time I stayed indoors, and I didn't feel like I was getting any better. At one stage I was convinced

I had ME, which I'd heard could take years to get better from. This was a reasonable assumption because I was exhausted all the time, and even mild activity left me feeling worn out, but I know now this was more due to my inactivity over the months and being housebound. I spent a lot of time indoors staring at screens too. I would watch TV for hours on end, or go on the computer, because sometimes it provided a distraction. It wasn't healthy though.

Looking back now I really don't know how I got through that time. I would wake up in the morning feeling intimidated by all those hours stretching out in front of me, not having a clue how I was going to fill them, then sometimes by the evening I'd feel a little more relaxed but this wouldn't last long. I'd start to worry about not being able to sleep, and how I would get through the night if I couldn't, and even if I did manage sleep I'd wake up all too soon and it would be morning, then I'd have another day to contend with. Every day was the same for months on end. I didn't want to be housebound. I really wanted to be out there enjoying my life, and I wanted to be doing the things I heard other people were doing. No-one understood why I couldn't. I knew that I couldn't while I was feeling the way I was, but I didn't know why. I never thought about ringing the Samaritans, or going to see a counsellor, because I thought you could only do those things if you felt suicidal. I just thought I'd have to somehow try and get through this on my own. I was waiting in vain for a doctor to tell me what was wrong with me, and none of them ever mentioned the possibility that this could be more mental than physical. Actually it was both. To be fair I couldn't really explain properly how I was feeling at the time, and the doctors could only work with what I brought to them. I do kind of wish though that one of them had realised there was something going on beyond the physical symptoms.

I basically had a breakdown. It was a burn out brought on by a few years of living an extremely unhealthy lifestyle, rushing around all the time, losing touch with who I really was and going through a few stressful events that I didn't deal with properly at the time. I don't know what it was that let me live something like a normal life again, but a change of scenery was what initially helped. I went on holiday to Scotland with my family in August that year, and being totally removed from my normal life allowed me the space to realise that I wasn't dying, I'd probably just needed some time out. Whilst there I went for a walk with my mum one day and got further than I expected. The next day I went again and got further still. I even managed to go on day trips with my family to the Orkney Islands, and to Loch Ness. I still wasn't myself by a long way, but then I hadn't been for years anyway. I'd been trying to be someone else to impress others, and so having this time out was my chance to rediscover who I was. I was still having trouble figuring it out, but when I got back from Scotland I was at least feeling like I was on the mend.

When I got back I kept walking with my mum every day. I wonder what she'd have thought if I'd been able to tell her then that in 10 years I'd be lining up for a 100 mile ultramarathon. I went back to Uni that September, but the anxiety was still a problem and I had to come back to my parents' house a few times. I still came home every weekend, because the main problem was having time on my hands. I'd stopped drinking, and during the whole summer I'd just been stuck indoors the whole time, so at this point if I had free time I just didn't know what to do with myself. I needed some kind of focus.

It came in, let's just say, an unexpected form. The best way I can explain it is just to tell the story. Bear in mind how ill I'd been, but even knowing that it's hard to believe this actually happened. In March 2004 I went to see the Libertines at Bristol Colston Hall with Joe, Bob and Sergio. We enjoyed the gig, then Sergio and Bob came to stay at my house. Joe was living just round the corner at this time and we'd been to his for a while but he had work in the morning. That night Bob was talking about Paul Simon's 'Graceland' album, and wasn't very complimentary about it. We laughed about it for some time, and then Bob said "Paul Simon's gonna find out about this and sue me."

That weekend I went home, as always, and went to Sergio's. To cut a long story short, we decided to imagine what would happen if Paul Simon really did sue Bob, and so we wrote some information about the 'scandal' on Sergio's computer, including some quotes from outraged celebrities, and others who were more supportive of Bob's plight. The piece de resistance was a petition to stop Paul Simon from suing Bob for 'Gross slander and aggravated deformation of character.' The idea was that I'd get some friends to sign it and then we'd present it to him when I had. Things took an interesting turn when I told people about it at the pub and my friend Vicky said it would be a bit of a silly petition if only a few people signed it. I asked her how many signatures I'd have to get before it could be considered serious, and she said 1,000.

I was a man on a mission. Between 10th March and 10th April 2004 I, David James Urwin, got 1,026 people to sign a pretend petition to stop the musician Paul Simon from suing my friend Robert Christopher Sainsbury. I went up to lots of strangers and got them to sign it. I went up to lots of people I knew at Uni and got them to sign it. It took over my life. I don't know what else to say, except that this genuinely happened. I did it. I feel like I should write a few thousand words to justify myself, but all I can say is that I really wanted to prove Vicky wrong, I really wanted to make Bob and Sergio laugh, and the upshot of all of this was that I had something to occupy my thoughts for an entire month, which meant that I forgot to be anxious for an entire month, which meant that my anxiety illness got better. It never got as bad as it was after this. I've had panic attacks since, but now I know what I'm dealing with and so it's never been as much of a problem. So there you have it. If you have a breakdown and are struggling to get better just get loads of people to sign a fictional petition. Miracle cure. Please note that this is not genuine medical advice, although it worked for me, so if literally all else fails why not give it a try?

Norfolk Coastal Ultra
(October 13th 2012)

After completing a 50 mile ultra in February the next logical step was to have a go at 62, which is 100 kilometres. Norfolk Coastal Ultra was a perfect choice, as I had been born in Norfolk of course, and would be returning to my homeland to try something quite challenging. Just before 8am I was lined up with 97 other ultra runners and around 40 marathoners at Kelling Heath Holiday Park, ready to start what I had been longing to start all week, and what had been in the back of my mind for some time before that. Among the ultra runners was one Sam Robson, who had run around 90 miles home after completing London Marathon the year before, and had since put in some impressive performances in ultra races, including a 2nd place finish at South Downs Way 100 four months before this race. I didn't know he was there at the time as I didn't know what he looked like, but I would later contact him to tell him he'd inspired me and have now met him a couple of times. He is known, to me, as the sideburned assassin and is a top bloke, as well as a very talented runner.

At the start I was chatting to a German lady who was running the marathon, and then race organiser Lee Fudge appeared out of nowhere and shouted "3....2....1....go!" er....Ok then. My friend Jan and her partner Carl, who live locally, were going to run the first couple of miles with me as Jan had originally planned to run the race but her training had been hampered by a couple of injuries. Carl had just gone to find a toilet and so I would have to start without them. This was also the last I saw of the German lady, which made me wonder if I was going too fast for quite a while. I stuck to what I felt was a sensible pace for the first few miles and she was somewhere behind me. Surely this couldn't be right if she was doing less than half the distance? Well never mind, a mantra I kept repeating to myself in the early stages was "Run your own race", and I meant this as a means of making sure I took it nice and slow, but I also felt I shouldn't go slower than seemed natural just because someone else was going slower than I was. Anyway, it was almost no time before Jan and Carl caught up with me and it was a massive help to have them run the first couple of miles. We chatted away and those first two miles through the woods seemed to disappear in no time. It was a shame to say goodbye to them, but before long I was properly into my stride and enjoying the picturesque North Norfolk coast, trying not to think about how far I still had left to go.

The route followed a track across some heathland and then onto the dreaded shingle beach section that I'd heard so much about. A number of runners seemed to be following the ridge at the top of the beach but a few others were lower down on an area that seemed to be compacted with vegetation. In the route description both of these options had been mentioned, and in a split second decision I opted for the lower ground. In the most part this seemed to be the right choice, as the surface underfoot was pretty true, but there came a time when I was forced up onto the ridge. I actually began to think this would have been a better option, as it was mostly nice and compacted too, but there were occasional stretches where it would give way to loose shingle and would slow us down a little. Mind you, with only five or six miles in the legs it didn't seem in the least bit harrowing.

Before long I was at the first checkpoint, which I ran straight through without stopping, and as I continued along coastal tracks, through Cley village and onto a fairly long path section I didn't want to get ahead of myself but I was beginning to feel pretty strong. For a while I ran with a guy from the RAF, who said he'd barely run in around four years and had never run more than 16 miles in one go before. I would later see him approaching the half-way point as I had just commenced my return journey from it, so I know he made it at least that far. Around 11 miles in the leader of the marathon went running back the other way. "Keep it going, mate. Looking strong" I said to him as he was approaching. As he looked up he said "Hey, I recognise you. You're famous." I laughed, and wondered where he might know me from. Perhaps from an article in Trail Running magazine about how I'd used running to help manage my depression, or perhaps he mistook me for someone else. Either way, little moments like this can act as a real boost. When I ran past my mum and dad and our friend Michael just after this my dad joked that the marathon leader was doing the ultra. If he had been he'd most definitely have been on course to smash the 100k world record.

At the second checkpoint I ate half a banana and told the marshalls "This is easy", and at that point I was only half joking. Up until the checkpoint at mile 20 I simply stayed in the zone and kept churning out the miles at a manageable pace. A few guys were running close behind me for a while and I had to tell them I didn't really know where I was going, just in case they were following me on purpose. The quarter way point passed with me still feeling full of running, and the coastal landscape seemed more and more inspiring all the time. That's one of the things I enjoy most about these races, as I mentioned before. It just makes everything all about the present moment, which can be so hard to find in this modern age where we are constantly bombarded with information. I chatted with a runner from Liverpool as we approached the 20 mile checkpoint, and we agreed that it was just starting to hurt a little bit but we both felt strong. We decided to run the approaching beach section together, and agreed that we didn't want to walk a single step until at least the marathon point. I was so lucky to have company on the beach section as where there was soft sand I could feel that the effort required to maintain a reasonable pace was creeping up all the time. This was a section that could easily have taken forever if my mind had wavered. Eventually we made it onto a slightly easier path through the dunes and then onto a boardwalk that led to Burnham Overy Staithe. Around half way along this path my new friend said that he'd have to walk for a little while and he'd see me at the checkpoint. I probably should have done the same, but I just wanted to get to the food, and so I kept running. By this point my legs were definitely beginning to feel the strain, but my mind still felt like titanium, like that song. That is a song, right? Anyway, little did I know that within less than a mile the wheels would come off, and here is one of many metaphors for life that you can find in an ultramarathon. Sometimes you don't see the low points coming.

So there I was with 36 miles still to go, and the very first situation I described in my introduction was happening. I was cramping up, and still had such a long way to go. I'd been eating salty pretzels though, and was slowing down, so I hoped it wouldn't be too long before I started to feel better. If I hadn't known about the effects of cramp I probably would have thought my race was over, but I knew that cramp indicated a lack of salt in the body, and so I was trying to do something about it. The main thing was not to panic, for as long as I reached a plateau and just kept up a sustained effort at anything above a stagger then mathematically my chances of finishing within the 14 hour cut-off were still looking good. The half-way point (technically past half-way point) seemed to take forever to arrive, but the cramp had gone by the time I got there, and the nausea I'd been feeling had mostly gone as well. I didn't get too excited as I begun the return leg though, as I knew the beach section was still to come. I remember little from this point until the beach section was nearly over, which suggests that it was just head down, grinding out the miles. Or maybe I sleep walked/ran it. Either way, I just beat the advancing tide to get round the edge of the last wooden groyne on the beach at Wells-next-the-sea, and my parents were there to greet me at the end of the beach. I now remember that my mum was starting to tell me something but then half way through I interrupted her and said "Must get to the checkpoint." It was only round the corner, and I kept running to get there. I didn't interrupt her intentionally, I was just so absorbed in the moment that I was fairly oblivious to what was going on around me. Sorry, mum.

The checkpoint volunteers asked me how I was feeling and I truthfully told them that I was feeling great, and was just so happy to have the beach section out of the way. I ate what I could and then set off on my way. At this point I was able to run at a fairly decent pace for quite some time unbroken. In fact when I got to the village of Blakeney a couple of miles later my mum said "Blimey, that was quick!" A little later I walked for a while with a guy named Will, who said that mentally he just didn't have the energy to run any more, but he thought he would still make the cut-off by walking fast. There came a time when I felt I had to start running again or I might not want to either, and as much as I was loving the experience I wanted to get this thing finished.

At the penultimate checkpoint Lee Fudge's wife told me it was only five miles until the next one, which was some truly enchanting music to my ears. I've always found the phrase 'music to my ears' a little odd, as the type of music is not specified and it's not necessarily a good thing. I had to high five her, as she was the most encouraging checkpoint volunteer I had ever met. Such things can make a huge difference in a race of this length. When you've been on your feet from soon after dawn until soon before dusk, and have covered more distance than many believe it's possible for a human being to cover in a day, a few kind words and a positive vibe can carry you a lot further.

I was still running pretty well at this point, and ran for a while with another guy I'd encountered at the checkpoint. He'd practically downed a cup of soup, which for some reason I found really quite impressive. We managed to miss a gap between two houses that led onto a path in Cley village, and so ended up having to climb over a fence. As you may be able to imagine, climbing over a fence when you've just run 55 miles isn't the easiest thing to do, or the most enjoyable thing to do, but we made it. As we approached the final checkpoint it was really beginning to get quite dark, but I didn't want to put on my head torch until we got there, or my lightweight windproof jacket. Once we arrived I realised that I was actually beginning to get pretty exhausted. I managed to put my jacket on inside out without realising at first, and I stuffed sweets in my mouth with a ferocity I hadn't at any other time in my adult life. I then got a bit confused as to where the exit to the car park was. However, once I was on the shingle beach I was back in the zone. The final section was just as memorable as that of the Thames Trot had been.

I knew that around three miles along the shingle beach was a pillbox, and when I reached it I had to head down the shingle mound and onto the home stretch. I also knew that around a mile before the pillbox my parents were going to be standing, and so at least I knew until I passed them I hadn't gone past the pillbox, which was my biggest fear. At first there was more loose shingle than I remembered there being on the way out, and I couldn't seem to find the compacted sections of the ridge. I actually said out loud to the shingle "Come on, I've run such a long way. Play fair", and would talk to myself quite a bit before the end. The shingle seemed to listen to me and before long I was on the ridge, but then I realised I had a stone in my shoe. "Oh, I don't care" I thought to myself. Ok, it might have hurt a bit but at this point I was in so much pain that I'd just got used to it, and so I'd deal with it at the end. I'd promised Boldebort I'd try and get her some kind of memento of this quest, and I wanted to get her some kind of interesting stone from the beach, because she loves the sea, and shells, and interesting pebbles. I saw a couple of possibilities but when I reached down to pick them up they just weren't right, and when I rose up again I felt a bit dizzy. I didn't want to leave the beach without an interesting stone, and so I briefly thought about just collapsing onto the shingle and looking around me until I found a decent one, but then I thought if any other runners passed me they might think I'd gone mad and call for help, and I was still against the clock. I couldn't wait for a detailed psychological assessment to take place. Just a few more steps and I spotted a stone that looked a bit like a shark's tooth. Result! I put it in my backpack and made for the torch beam I could see in the distance. Pretty soon after this I realised that actually I did care about the stone in my shoe, and so I momentarily sat on a rock and took my shoe off to get it out.

A heap of sand tumbled out of my as well, which I'd forgotten was even in there. I didn't bother with my other shoe though.

There's something so incredible about running at night away from civilisation. It's a sensory overload, especially if you've been out all day and are feeling kind of high from the fatigue, and the truckload of endorphins. As I made my way along that shingle ridge with the waves crashing to my left, a beam of light up ahead and a few stars dotted around among the clouds in the night sky above I felt an incredible sense of connectedness with myself that modern life, with all of its distractions, so often robbed me of. But was this only because I allowed it to? In that moment I was reminded who I am, and where I feel most at peace, which is out surrounded by nature. In the moment I promised myself that I would try and embrace this more each day, if only by making sure I went for at least a short stroll outdoors every single day, or by taking five minutes to sit outside and take some deep breaths when I woke up in the morning, or before going to bed at night. When I was actually in the moment though I wasn't really thinking any of this, I was just right there and I wasn't really thinking about anything much at all. It was only when reflecting on it afterwards that I realised what a contrast it was from my usual day to day life.

Anyway, I found my parents and gratefully took a handful of jelly babies, then I made my way back off into the darkness, swinging the beam of my headtorch up and down the beach, desperately searching for that pillbox. The next section seemed to take literally the whole of my life up to that point all over again, and negative thoughts began to peck at me like malignant crows, but then at last the pillbox came into view. Or did it? I swore I could see it, but it seemed to get no closer no matter how far I scrambled my way along the shingle towards it. Where was it? Oh crikey! All of a sudden I realised that it wasn't the pillbox I was seeing, but the distant outline of the coast further along. However, at the very instant I recognised this the pillbox materialised in front of me. I laughed out loud at this for some time, as wave after wave of euphoria cascaded over me. I looked down and saw a glowstick attached to a rock that led to the beginning of the final stretch. As I began to jog down the path I just couldn't stop laughing. At this point I knew I was going to make it. What a monstrously epic day it had been, and it was going to end in triumph.

Unfortunately, as often seems to happen, the realisation that I was going to make it meant my legs decided they could stop pretending to be fine and were able to tell me how they really felt. Oh come on, legs. Don't you have a bit more emotional intelligence than that? Can't you wait until I've crossed the finish line? Please? "No, Dave. I don't think you even begin to understand what you've put us through today. We used to like you more when you were a wreckhead and you didn't do any of this running nonsense." Well if my legs weren't going to listen to my pleas then I figured I may as well just slow down and take it all in. I'm so glad I did, because as I trudged through that forest in the night, occasionally stumbling across a glowstick to show me the way, and an owl flying across my path at one point, I felt like I was in a fairytale, following a trail of breadcrumbs through an enchanted forest. Things like this tend to stay with me, and can act as emotional armour against the slings and arrows of outrageous fortune that will inevitably appear in life. I thought about so many things during that final mile or two, but foremost in my mind was that on this day I had the strength to do something that not everyone would. Maybe that was because many people would have felt like they had nothing to prove when they cramped up and felt sick at mile 26, and would have been quite happy to stop, going back to their normal life quite happy to not to have run another step, but really this was about wanting to achieve something that once seemed impossible, and making it happen whatever the obstacles.

So yes, after a couple of road crossings, a railway line crossing and a short climb up a track through some heathland I found myself on the paved surface that told me I was at the holiday park, and must be near the finish line. I tried to summon up one last effort to finish strongly, and as I rounded a corner I thought I could see two figures in high visibility jackets up ahead. Then I heard applause. Every last ounce of energy I had was sent to my legs, and I increased the pace, building to a semi-sprint finish. I was born in Norfolk, and when I saw my parents at the finish line a thought crossed my mind as to whether they might ever have imagined back then that one day they'd be watching me do something like this. I crossed the line, stood tall and raised my arms, then fell to my knees. I heard someone ask if I was Ok, and I gave them a thumbs-up as I raised my head, a massive smile breaking out across my face. The next day I had a sense of déjà vu as I could barely walk up and down the stairs, and was utterly exhausted all day, eating and drinking everything in sight.....well, at least anything edible or drinkable, and I tried to take a brief stroll around the village in the hope that my legs wouldn't sieze up permanently. For the record I beat the cut-off by an hour-and-a-half, and finished 28th overall, which isn't bad. I was so proud of what I'd achieved but I totally believed, as I do now, that anyone who could run could get to the point where they could do it if they really wanted to.

The next weekend I took part in a race called Exmoor Stagger, organised by Minehead Running Club. It's about 16 miles and features a climb from sea level up to the top of Dunkery Beacon, Somerset's highest 'mountain', and then back again a different way. I managed to finish, and my legs had been pretty tired but I still managed a respectable enough time. I took two tumbles during the race, the first was coming off the top of Dunkery Beacon, when I slipped and my legs went from under me and I landed right on my bum. I got straight back up though, and the worse fall was two miles from the end, where I tripped on a stone and went flying over, grazing my knee to smithereens. I would later get this cleaned up by St. John's Ambulance staff, but not before I'd finished the race, and the adrenaline certainly made the last couple of miles quicker. I was very pleased though to see the two runners who were immediately ahead of me stop to check if I was Ok when it had happened. This is the right kind of spirit, and one that I always try and bring to each race I enter. Besides, the welfare of the other runners far outweighs any personal goals, as should be the case in life, replacing 'runners' with 'people'. Before long I was ready to start planning my next challenge. I wanted to take on something that was considered properly tough by your average ultra runner. What would it be?

Time to Live

When I finally felt free of my anxiety illness I thought about all those months I'd spent feeling imprisoned, just like I had at school, and promised myself I would do everything I could to make the most of my life. When I'd been ill I'd read a lot of books, many of them travel writing, and had decided I wanted to see a bit of the world. I hadn't really had a clue what to do after leaving Uni, and the idea of having the next few years mapped out with adventure seemed perfect, and so I planned to save as much money as I could and then go inter-railing around Europe. After that I'd come back, save some more and then travel round the world. For someone who'd spent the best part of seven months barely leaving the house this seemed ludicrous, but I felt so much better now and I was pretty fearless. That was until I read about the possible dangers there could be in any of the places I would be travelling to. For "There are pickpockets" I read "This town is infested with pickpockets, who will take everything you have if you turn your back for a second." For "Occasional violent crimes against travellers have been reported" I read "You will be beaten to death. There is no avoiding it." Such warnings really put me off going to certain places, and I was mainly seeking out places that were reported as being safe. The things I was most excited about were walking up mountains in Norway, round lakes in Slovenia and along coast paths in Iceland. Basically I was up for lots of time out in nature, with the occasional foray into a town to get a bit of the old culture.

These were very different times to those we live in today. If you weren't all that fussy about what you did there were temporary jobs all over the place. You could literally pick up the odd day's work here and there if you wanted it, or could go and work in a factory for a while until you got bored and then go and work in another one. In saving to travel round Europe I worked in a factory making vacuum cleaners, in another one making air filters for cars, doing telemarketing for a gym, washing dishes in a couple of schools, waiting tables at a New Year's Eve do at a golf club, promoting a newspaper in a supermarket and I think some other things that I can't even remember. I also helped at the Royal Mail sorting office over Christmas, and would work crazy shifts, starting at 4pm and then finishing at 6 the next morning. I didn't care about the long hours, because I knew the more I worked the more money I'd have for my travels. I was young and it seemed like such a simple equation. When work finished I tried to spend as much time as possible hanging out with friends, whilst any spare time I had I was planning for my adventures. I was planning to travel on my own, partly because I didn't know anyone else who had the same plans, but partly because I'd travelled so far inside my own head during all those months spent in the house that I found it hard to spend too much time with other people. Also, not drinking any more and going back to Uni, where the lifestyle was built around drinking, meant that I struggled to fit in. I could handle being around drunk people still at this point though. One night when I'd done a DJ set in Bristol my housemate Ross and me came back to my house with our friend Rachael. They were both pretty trolleyed and I was completely sober but we were trying to get our taxi driver to sing Justin Timberlake with us on the way back and I was fully involved, then we were playing The Darkness at full blast in my room at 4am, cheering and clapping when the song finished. I was able to behave like a drunk person just by being around them.

I was definitely busy, and it didn't even occur to me that I might burn out again. There was only one time I was close to it, but I recognised the signs, and so I took the next week off work and went to the Isles of Scilly for a few days, then went to visit Bob at Uni in Exmouth for a couple more. Basically I just needed a break from my normal routine, and I'd later realise just how rejuvenating the Isles of Scilly could be, but back then they were just somewhere I could find a bit of peace and quiet. There wasn't much peace and quiet at Bob's, there were drama students on magic mushrooms, but one of them made me a cheese toastie at 2am as we chatted about life and so I could cope. Of course

I'd stopped drugs and booze completely at this point, had done for some time, but I could go without much in the way of sleep because I had such a lease of life from being well again. I think we got about an hour's sleep that night, and then in the morning we walked into town and rounded a corner to see a brass band coming towards us. It was too much for us in our groggy state, and we looked at each other, screamed and ran away.

Not long after that I had a surreal but fun experience as a contestant on the popular Channel 4 game show Countdown. Channel 4 paid for me to get a train up to Leeds and stay at the Holiday Inn Express, which at the time I thought was the swankiest hotel you could get. On the show I came up against the series champion in my first game, and I put up a fight worthy of my tough, Geordie heritage. It got down to the final round, the conundrum, and whoever spotted it first would win. He spotted it first.

I'm not sure how differently my life would have turned out if I'd beaten him, but I'm fairly sure I would have beaten the next person in line. About five episodes a day are filmed, and that would have been the last one, so I would have had to come back the next day and film some more. That would have meant the next day would have panned out differently to how it did, and so in theory every subsequent day would have panned out differently too. I wonder just how much of a difference it would have made. Would I ever have got into running? Would my European travels have been massively different? Would I ever have met the people I have since that day? There is no way of ever knowing, but it makes me wonder why things pan out the way they do, and how it's possible that every single decision we make alters the course of our future massively. I'd had similar thoughts as a very young child, and this had felt like a lot of pressure at the time. Do I believe that everything happens for a reason? We'll get to that all in good time.

The time came to set off on my travels and I couldn't wait to get going. A few days before I went I'd performed my first stand-up comedy set at an open mic night in Exmouth. It had been an interesting experience. I'd had HP sauce squirted in my face by a member of the audience who I'd spoken to. I thought the only way I could save any dignity from the situation would be to tell him he was wonderful and kiss him on the cheek, so I did. It basically worked. My material was pretty poor I think, but I got a buzz from being in front of the audience. Being so introverted, it was totally against my character to do stand-up, but then many performers say they do it to combat shyness. I guess with me I was still putting on an act to a degree, but instead of silly drunken antics I was completely sober. I suppose again after recovering from the breakdown I just felt so alive, and wasn't afraid of the worst thing that could happen if something went wrong, at least when it came to performing onstage.

I set off from Bristol airport to Geneva, and it had been surreal to see policemen walking about with guns at the airport. I'd never seen a policeman carrying a gun before, and it just felt like something I was looking at on TV. The plane journey I'd found amazing, the feeling of going above the clouds and looking down on them made me turn to the guy in the seat next to me and say "Does that ever stop being impressive?" He shook his head. When I arrived in Switzerland my initial thought, knowing I would be out on the road for three months, was "What do people do when they travel, then?" I'd committed to coming out and travelling on my own for all this time assuming I'd just know what to do when I got there, but it took a while to get into the swing of things.

My first night I felt pretty lonely at first, but I was staying in a backpackers' hostel, as I would all the way round, and so it wasn't long before I met other travellers. I ended up chatting to a Cambodian guy who'd had to move to Europe to escape Pol Pot's Khmer Rouge regime, because if he hadn't he would have been murdered. Simple as that. I found it incredible, coming from England, that anyone would ever have to leave their homeland in order to save their life if they'd done nothing wrong. Even though our government didn't always seem like they had everyone's best interests at heart at least I didn't have any immediate fears of them shooting me. We were talking also to a man who lived in Uzbekistan but was originally from Georgia. He was keen to tell us his philosophy on life, which was basically that we're all the same but our life circumstances and the experiences we go through lead to our differences. This was similar to something I'd been thinking since my late teens, which was that almost all of the negativity in the world is due to a lack of understanding. Something I still essentially believe now. The Cambodian guy, whose name I have long forgotten, as is often the way it seems with people met on travels, also talked about how little elderly people are respected in the West compared to the East. How in Europe many old people are put in homes where they're out of the way and in the East they are always looked after by their families. In general this was the way it went. I would have interesting conversations with strangers, then a couple of days later I'd move to a different place, probably never to see those people again. It was an exciting way to live, but I wondered for how long it would be sustainable.

Something in Geneva that seemed to bear out the Georgian guy's philosophy was when I was on the top floor of an art gallery, where there was a window that allowed you to look out over the whole city, lake Geneva stretching out to sweeping mountain ranges. There's a 60 foot jet of water constantly shooting into the sky, which is visible just about anywhere you are nearby, and on that day there was a rainbow behind it. A German family came into the room while I was there, and then an Argentinian man with his young daughter, followed by some locals, and each of their reactions on seeing the view out of the window was the same. No matter where you're from in the world a stunning view is a stunning view.

Something that took a bit of getting used to in Switzerland was how every driver would slow down to let me cross the road in front of them. Everyone was just so polite and helpful. This had been a good place to start my travels as within a couple of days I felt at ease. My grip on my wallet loosened, and before long I was full of confidence in my new surroundings. Another thing that took some getting used to in Europe though was how the trains were always on time. One morning in Zagreb, Croatia, I got to the station a minute after my train to Hungary was due to leave and saw it pulling away as I arrived. I hadn't had any breakfast, and I decided to jump on a train to Ljubljana, the Slovenian capital, and get a connection to Budapest from there. To cut a long story short, I ended up spending an entire day on trains on which I couldn't get any food and so I was very hungry in Hungary. I finally arrived around 9pm that evening and didn't have a clue where my hostel was that I was planning to stay at. After nearly getting run over by a tram and trying to explain to an irate Hungarian man, neither of us speaking a word of the others' language, that I didn't have any cigarettes (he had said 'roken', which I knew was something to do with smoking in some language or another from the text on duty free packets of rolling tobacco) I heard an Irish accent and so I asked the guy if he knew where the street my hostel was on was. He was a student, and said he'd walk with me to where he thought it was, and eventually I managed to find it.

I'd still not eaten, and just thought I'd get some sleep and then have a proper feast in the morning. Unfortunately the Japanese guy who was the only other person in my dorm room wanted to talk. Quite a lot. I was feeling pretty faint, and was desperate for it to be the next morning so I could get something to eat, but his questions were relentless. I wouldn't have minded if I was on anything but an empty stomach, and if I'd known then what I did the next day I would have known that there were 24 hour shops aplenty in Budapest, but at that point I had no idea.

Eventually sleep came, and the next morning, after a substantial breakfast, I set out to explore the Hungarian capital. Men kept approaching me on the street trying to sell me different things, including binoculars, but they were all respectful and would take no for an answer straight away, which seemed to change the further east I got. During my travels I walked everywhere, and built up a decent level of hiking fitness as well as getting used to being on my feet all day. This was possibly the beginning of my physical preparation for running ultramarathons. There was one particular day in the Czech Republic when I set out in the morning and just kept hiking, thinking I'd turn back soon. It got later and later and eventually there came a time when I thought if I didn't turn back now I'd probably have to find somewhere to sleep outdoors for the night. I tried to walk back the way I came, setting myself different targets to be at a certain point by a certain time along the way and missing all of them by some minutes. It was dark before I got back, but spending the whole day outdoors and moving under my own power had made me feel so alive. It also made dinner taste exquisite because I'd worked up such an appetite.

I was a vegetarian when travelling, as I was for sixteen years from just before I left school, and vegetarianism isn't common in some places around Europe. In the Czech Republic all of the vegetarian dishes on the menus had ham in them, as if it wasn't real meat, apart from fried, battered cheese. In Budapest one day I decided to have some minestrone soup for lunch, after reading the description 'A marriage of vegetables' on the menu. I'd never been to a vegetable wedding but I'd guessed that no meat would be invited. I was wrong. In Iceland I had been stunned to see whale, puffin and guillemot on the menu. I've still not tried any of these but I have been told that whale meat is delicious, and is more like venison than any kind of fish. By the way yes, I do know that a whale is classed as a mammal. I'm still not sure I'd like to eat any of these things, mind. Could I really bring myself to eat a puffin? I am such a meat eater now that my mate Max has said he's worried I'll try and start gnawing on his leg, but I have my limits. Also, because I wasn't drinking, and didn't really want to go into detail about why, I spent the whole of my travels pretending I was allergic to alcohol. People asked a few questions about it and said it must be terrible, but they accepted it as a reason for me not drinking, which was all I needed.

Whilst in Budapest I also met two Americans called Matt and Jen, and ended up travelling through Romania with them for a week or so. After all that time on my own, although I was meeting people all the time, it was so nice to have a bit of continuity and to share the experience with a couple of others. Romania was a land of contrasts. On the train journeys it seemed like half of the countryside was a landfill site, and this also seemed to be the way in many of the towns, with every river full of plastic bottles and empty crisp packets, and yet the scenery was some of the most beautiful I encountered anywhere on my travels. Transylvania was full of pine forests and reminded me in places of the Scottish Highlands. There were packs of stray dogs wandering around in the town squares, and when the rain fell one day in the town of Cluj-Napoca it was like the streets were flooded within half an hour, as there wasn't much in the way of a drainage system, but the traffic lights of all things were far more high tech than in England, and even counted down in large digital numbers so that you would know when they were about to change. At that time they still had the old currency of Lei, of which you could withdraw 1 million from a cashpoint and it would be around 20 quid. I was a multi-millionaire.

Also in Romania I found that the people would look at me like I'd just saved their lives if I used a tiny bit of their language. I guess in England we don't become multi-lingual out of necessity, which people do in most other countries. No-one would have much reason to learn Romanian unless they are going to live there, so I guess people appreciate it when you make the effort. In the town of Oradea, not far over the border from Hungary, this wasn't so much the case, and it's probably partly because many people there still consider themselves to be Hungarian rather than Romanian. A couple of local girls we spoke to on the train said that they did, and also had nothing good to say about the sizeable local Roma population, known as gypsies. "They smell, they steal, they can't be trusted" was one of the more polite things I remember them saying. When they did I imagined Hungarian travellers on a bus in England speaking to some local teenage girls who were complaining about 'pikeys.' I guess things are probably the same the world over. Going back to the languages, we'd met a Romanian guy earlier on the same train who'd said it was his eightieth birthday.

"Me? I speak four languages. Romanian, English, German, Hungarian. You Americans you speak one language. No good."

"Parlez-vous francais?" I said to him, after we'd humoured him for a while.

"No" he said, shaking his head.

"Ah. No good" I smiled. Matt and Jen cracked up, and the poor man walked out of the carriage looking deflated. I was proud of my joke, but felt bad that maybe he hadn't taken it as one. He came back a minute or two later and all was good.

I had a great laugh with Matt especially. At breakfast the following morning he'd said "Hey, do you think this water's alright?" at the exact moment I was taking a sip of some tea. I caught his eye and he saw the expression on my face, starting to laugh. I don't know to this day how I managed to swallow that mouthful of tea but as soon as I did I gasped for air and then laughed so hard I could barely breathe. We tried to explain this to some people the next day, but as with so many things I found hilarious they never seemed as funny to other people who heard about them. The people I've felt closest to in my life have always been people who've shared my strange sense of humour. If you can laugh with someone there's very few arguments that can't be resolved.

Apart from Romania my favourite place was probably Iceland. There are very few trees there, and the landscape is extremely rugged, but to me this lends it a unique kind of beauty. Travelling there is pretty expensive because they have to import nearly everything, so I was glad I'd saved it for the end of my trip. I'd travelled there by ferry from Norway, via the Faroe Islands and Shetland Islands. I'd stayed in the Shetlands for just over a week, spending a few days on Fair Isle half way through, and being the only person apart from the crew who wasn't sick on the notoriously rough boat crossing. Fair Isle had a population of only sixty, and was a tiny island. For half the time I was there it rained, but I loved it. There was something for me about life seeming so much more real, and so much less stressful, when I could walk anywhere, where I would see the same people every day and would enjoy their company but would be allowed my own space if I wanted it. There was a colony of puffins living on the cliffs a minute's walk from the bird observatory, where I was staying, and the local Great Skuas, think of a fat seagull with mostly black feathers, would swoop down and fly right over my head if I got too close to their nesting area. I was surrounded by nature at its most simple, most wild and most atmospheric and I was sad to leave. Iceland would be much like this though, but on a larger scale, especially the village of Borgafjordir Eystri, where I would stay for a few days.

In Iceland in June the sun never sets. It gets a little gloomy for an hour or two just after midnight but it never gets properly dark, and that means when out walking you never have to worry how long you're out for as long as you have waterproofs. You'll be able to see where you're going no matter what time it is. In Borgafjordir Eystri I walked for miles around the rough cliff paths and up the nearby mountains. Sometimes it would start snowing or raining but this would never last long and then it would be a glorious summer's day again. It's not uncommon to have four seasons in a day. One of the main reasons I'd come to this place was because I knew there was a Steller's Eider, a magnificently coloured duck that had always been one of the birds I most wanted to see when I was a twitcher, somewhere in the area. I'd exchanged a few e-mails with an Icelandic birder before I came and he said at this time of year it might be up river a bit, so on my first day there I'd planned to take a long walk up the river and see what I could see. Before long it had started snowing quite heavily, so I decided to walk back and have some lunch first, but as I was nearing the hostel I saw something out in the bay and raised my binoculars, as I had when I saw that Snowy Owl on the Cairngorms years before, and there it was. The Steller's Eider was a couple of minutes' walk from where I was staying. Around it were a flock of the arguably even more impressive Harlequin Ducks, which are common in Iceland but which many twitchers in the UK would travel the length of the island to see. A couple of small wading birds fluttered across the harbour. They were Red-necked Phalaropes (look them up on the old google images if you feel like it.)

It was a bit of a shame to go to Reykjavik after being somewhere so wonderfully wild and remote, that was full of mind-blowing nature, but I enjoyed my time in Iceland's capital. The highlight was probably going out on a boat and seeing Minke whales. Again the experiences with nature were some of the most memorable. I also met some fun people at the hostel, although I scared an Australian guy when I explained to him what 'glassing' was, including a dramatic interpretation.

"You look like you've done that before, mate!" he stammered.

"Oh no," I laughed, "I'm the least likely person to do that ever." I don't know if he believed me.

Finally it was time to come back to England, and I tried to make it a complete surprise for my parents, but when I got back they'd gone to visit some friends in Norfolk. Luckily next door were in and they had a spare key. I'd also tried to surprise Joe in Bath before I went back home, but one of his friends had seen me and hadn't realised it was meant to be a surprise I was back, so I was foiled time and time again. At least I managed to surprise Sergio, turning up unannounced in the pub where he worked. He ran out from behind the bar and hugged me, which is the kind of welcome home I'd been hoping for everywhere, because I knew the novelty of me being back would wear off before long. I felt like a different person for a while on my return. Having to get by completely on my own, including in places I didn't speak a word of the language, had given me a lot more confidence. Mind you, in Iceland I'd gone over my overdraft limit and had returned with no money, no job, no girlfriend and no immediate plans. I had to live with my parents and look for another poorly paid job to try and get some money together again, and before too long it was almost like I'd never been away. It was great to see all my family and friends again, and live something like a normal life for a while, but they all had their own lives and I still had no real clue what I wanted to do with mine. If I was to go away again I wouldn't have to decide.

Jurassic Coast ONER
(20th April 2013)

After 100 kilometres the next common distance for ultras is 100 miles, but before I had a go at that there was one race that leapt out at me more than any other. The Jurassic Coast was the place that had possibly been responsible for my love of the outdoors more than anywhere else. My parents brought Joe and me down for walks at Charmouth and Seatown from a very early age, and I remember Seatown being my favourite place for some time. Golden Cap, a challenging walk from Charmouth, was somewhere we often came as well. When training for my first Three Peaks Challenge I spent one late summer's day walking as far as I felt like from Charmouth before turning back and walking back the other way. I made it to West Bexington, which I think is about 13 miles, and by the time I got back it was pitch black. I'd walked inland from Seatown and alongside the busy main road back into Charmouth because I hadn't brought a torch with me. My legs had been complaining most of the way back, and the climb up to the beacon above West Bay I can remember feeling like it was never going to end. In late 2010 Boldebort and me walked from Charmouth to Weymouth to raise money for Mind. This still remains one of my favourite ever days, purely because I've rarely laughed so much as I did then, and we spent the whole day from dawn until dusk outdoors in stunning surroundings. It took us all day though, and we were exhausted by the end of it. Not long after that I learnt of something called the Jurassic Coast Challenge, where participants run from Charmouth to Weymouth one day, then from Weymouth round the isle of Portland and then on to Lulworth Cove the next, and then on the third day they run from Lulworth Cove to Studland, basically a coastal marathon per day. Then for the unbelievably hardcore there's the Jurassic Coast ONER, which is all of that in 24 hours.

When I heard of the ONER I thought it would be fun to give it a go one day, but wasn't sure if I'd ever be in a position to. In August

2011 I took part in the Dorset Doddle, which is a 32 mile event from Weymouth to Swanage organised by Dorset Long Distance Walking Association. Some people run it, treating it as a roughly 50 kilometre ultramarathon, and I had that intention. What I hadn't bargained for was how many colossal climbs and descents there would be, and in the end the whole thing took me nearly 8 hours, which would work out at about four miles per hour. If the course was totally flat I'd fancy my chances of walking every step in that kind of time. I had to work the next day, but ended up going home early because I was just exhausted. So basically if I wanted to do the ONER I'd have to do what Boldebort and me did, then a circuit of Portland, then the whole of the Dorset Doddle course, plus about another 10k on the end, and considerably quicker than I'd done it before. All of it. No chance.

At least that's what I thought in 2011, but in 2012 I'd run 50 miles in a day, and then 62, and so I began to think why not 80 odd? The two previous ultras I'd done had been on flat courses, and this would be anything but. Late in 2012 though I signed up, and paid my money, so all that remained was to try and make sure I was in some kind of shape to give it a go. I did a fair bit of training on the actual course with my parents, who are both retired by the way, acting as my support crew. I broke it up into different sections, and did the training in February and March 2013. It had been an especially harsh and wet winter, and so much of the Coast Path was a bit of a quagmire to be honest. I was quite pleased in a way, because if there were muddy conditions on race day I'd be prepared, and if the conditions were much better it would be easier than during my training. Some of the mud was so deep, squelchy and slippery as to make it pretty un-runnable, but worse than this was one particular day when there was snow, high winds and a wind chill factor of about -7. I started in Weymouth and the first mile I was running into a ferocious headwind, which meant I was working much harder than I should have been straight away. For much of the way there was snow hitting me in the face, and so I was trying to keep my head down but still look where I was going. I slipped and fell once or twice on a snowy field, then my gloves had got covered in snow that melted and seeped through, making my hands feel like they were frostbitten. There are some massive climbs on this part of the route, and when they're thick with mud they're even more challenging than usual. Approaching Lulworth Cove there are three massive, steep climbs in a row, each followed by a massive, steep descent, and when I got to these I naturally slowed down quite a bit. On a day as cold as it was this really wasn't what I needed, and I was beginning to feel a little chilly. I've never been so relieved to hear gunfire as I was then, as I knew it meant I wasn't far from the car park at Lulworth Cove, which is right next to an army firing range. I don't think I've ever moved so quickly towards the sound of gunfire either. There's a massive, gentle downhill slope towards the car park, which meant I was able to run at a decent pace and look like I was in control of things. When I got to the bottom though I got straight in my parents' car and asked if they would drive me a little further down the coast so I could do a different section, mostly because I just wanted a chance to warm up. It was tempting not to get out of the car again but I did, and covered a fair bit more distance. If I hadn't stopped to warm up though in between I'd probably have been at risk of hypothermia.

In the lead-up to the race I'd run a half-marathon PB of 1 hour, 36 minutes at Taunton Half-Marathon, and was really happy with how my training had been going. I was extremely lucky with the weather conditions on the day, a week or so of sunshine and wind prior to the event drying out the coast path quite a bit, and then on the day it wasn't too hot but was sunny enough. Registration was at Ferrybridge, on the edge of Weymouth, and then we would be taken to the start at Charmouth on a minibus. When I was checking in some students who were making a film to promote the event asked me if I'd mind doing a little interview. I thought why ever not, and answered the questions with a mixture of seriousness and humour. I enjoyed telling them about the 'staircase of death', a massive flight of steps going down one cliff and then another massive flight of steps going back up the cliff on the other side, which was just before St.Aldhelm's head, about 60 miles in. I imagined this might take about an hour during the race because my legs would be so battered by then, and I planned to get there with plenty of time to spare.

Race organiser Ben Mason did an entertaining speech before the start, telling us that three types of people did the ONER. The first lot would be looking strong near the beginning, and then would continue to look strong throughout. These would usually be professional ultra runners. The second lot would look strong early on, but then fall apart somewhere during the second marathon and would drop out. The third lot would be the same as the second lot, but they'd make it to the finish because they'd listened to what he'd said during the briefing. He reminded us that we had 24 hours, and so we should use them. We should power-hike the uphills, run the downhills and run/walk the flat sections mostly, and that would be enough to let us finish under the cut-off. Also that if he said we had to drop out we would be dropping out, and he had his boxing gloves with him in case anyone argued. I don't think he was joking.

On the minibus to the start I chatted to the other runners, and everyone seemed a little nervous. There was a guy named Tom who'd done the race the previous year and had to drop out due to sickness at around mile 50. I was one of a number of first-timers, and we all said similar things. Basically we were all there to complete it, and would take it easy from the start and make sure we were moving just fast enough to beat the cut-off. However, beneath this I had an ambitious goal of finishing in under 20 hours. I thought this might be possible if everything went to plan, and was going to run my own race and see what happened.

The start was incredibly low-key. My club mate Rob had come to watch the start but he hadn't been able to find it because there wasn't even an Adventure Hub (the race organiser) flag anywhere at the car park. I managed to catch up with him quickly before we set off, and was extremely grateful for him being there, as my parents were once again. We had an electronic 'dibber', which had to be 'dibbed' at each checkpoint along the route, along with a band having to be removed from our backpacks, and to start we had to dib a box that Ben was wearing around his neck. Any massively unrealistic thoughts I'd had of winning the race evaporated within less than a minute of the start as Adam Holland, who held the world record of being the youngest man to ever run 100 marathons, which he'd done by the age of 23, disappeared off up the first climb like a mountain goat. He didn't really slow down the whole way and comfortably won the race. At one point he'd been on course for finishing in around 15 hours, but then a slight injury meant he eased off a little bit for the last 20 miles or so and in the end finished in about 17.

I was 4th for a while early in the race, and was running with a guy named Nigel for much of the first 20 miles. It was a gloriously sunny day, and the Jurassic Coast is no doubt one of the most stunning locations in the UK, and so I couldn't have been much happier. I would pull away from Nigel a little on the climbs, but he'd catch up pretty easily on the downhills and then we'd run together and chat for a while. He repeated quite often that he felt we'd be able to keep up the same pace all the way. I wasn't so sure, and thought I'd definitely slow down a lot in the second half, but it was nice to have the company. All was well until about 15 miles in, when the heat of the day made me just start to feel a little bit queasy. I was able to keep going through it for a while, but then when we reached check point 3 at Langton Herring I told Nigel to keep going and I'd hopefully catch up in a while. If I hadn't done this I'd have been drawn into his race, which is something I'd told myself I wouldn't be doing. I had to run my own race. That would be how I'd finish this thing.

The next section along the Fleet to Weymouth was a bit of a trial. I kept having to slow down, and was passed by a number of people. I wasn't worried though, because I knew there was a long, long way to go and as long as I looked after myself I'd feel better in a while. When I got to Weymouth I told my parents that I was just running my own race and was feeling good. At the checkpoint I saw a guy in a Yeovil Town Road Runners vest and told him I was also from Somerset. There were actually two runners from Yeovil in the race. The first, Lee Harwood, would end up finishing 3rd in his first ultra, which was a stunning performance. The second, Mike Harvey, would end up becoming a big part of my race.

On the isle of Portland I started to do what you should never do early in an ultra and thought about how far there was still to go. On one of the bigger climbs I started to get a little cramp in my quads. Again I didn't panic, because I'd overcome similar problems before, but I knew there were some humungous climbs still to come in the second half, and I'd wanted to have plenty of time in the bank to take them on. Luckily the cramp faded pretty quickly, and I was able to run pretty well along the West Cliffs. Lee passed me there after a brief chat, and I just started to think once again how lucky I was to be able to experience this. Really there's not much better than running or walking surrounded by awe inspiring nature. I'd always felt this, even when I tried to pretend it wasn't true, and now I'd battled back from the edge of the void to get to a level of fitness where I could attempt something that anyone would agree was a proper challenge. In terms of my overall life position a lot could be better, but none of that mattered for a second right now. It could wait, and I was on the way towards getting to where I wanted to be. For now it was time to enjoy the present.

I pretended to be an aeroplane when running towards the checkpoint half way round Portland. My dad told me to stop showing off, but I really wasn't. I was just free of inhibitions and off my face on endorphins. It was just like when I'd been wasted back in the dark times of my youth, but it was so much better than any artificial high could ever be. I was alive. I asked for some salt to help with the cramp, and the volunteer said I should dissolve some in a cup of coke, which I did. The salt tasted amazing, which was a sure sign I needed it. "Do you need anything else?" they asked. "Just a high five" I replied, and high fived everyone before setting off on my way again.

My dad told me a little further up the road that Lee and a couple of others weren't far ahead. "It doesn't matter where they are" I said straight away, but it was me I was trying to convince more than him. While I was feeling good it was difficult not to get drawn back into racing, but I wasn't even half way yet, and so it was all about looking after myself and moving forward at a comfortable pace. As the first signs of dusk appeared in the air I ran past a dog walker on the cliff path. His dog tried to go for my water bottle and I said "Nah dog, mate. You wouldn't like this; it's an electrolyte replacement drink." The owner seemed to find this hilarious and I was so happy to think of him recounting the story to people later on. I was feeling so strong at this point, but still took it easy on the climb up to Verne prison, stopping for a moment to take in the view across the Fleet when I reached the top of the hill. It was getting dark by this point, and there was a carpet of artificial lights down below, with the outline of the waves still visible beyond the shoreline. The air was still warm enough, and I couldn't stop smiling to myself.

When I was running back along the road to Weymouth the film crew from earlier drove past and sounded their horn, giving me plenty of encouragement. When I got back to the checkpoint I was chatting to everyone, and I think race director Ben was taken aback by how jolly I was. I tried some more salt but it tasted dreadful, which meant my electrolyte balance was all good. I wanted to keep pushing on while I felt good, and I knew the next few miles were pretty flat, so I kept moving and before long had caught up with a group of runners on the edge of Weymouth Town Centre. "Hey guys, looking strong" I said, and a couple of them recognised me from when they'd passed me on the fleet earlier. "You're getting stronger as you go on, aren't you?" said one of them, laughing. I quickly decided I'd run with them for a while. There were two Toms, the one from the bus earlier and another who seemed to have a lot of pace in his legs still, and there was James, who was a former soldier and a colossus of a man. We ran through town being shouted at by groups of drunk women, and I laughed at how years ago I'd have been on the other side thinking the runners were insane, and that there was no better way to spend your time than drinking. How things had changed.

On the other side of town we bumped into Mike, and he decided to run with us as well. The second Tom went off ahead after a while, just as the first Tom started to slow up a bit, and I briefly considered going off ahead too but I thought it might be good to have some company for a while. I began to regret my decision just slightly as it became obvious that Tom was really struggling. I wanted to get to at least the next checkpoint before I thought about deserting him, because I knew it might be dangerous for him on the section approaching Lulworth Cove if he didn't keep moving, but in the back of my mind were bad thoughts of how he might slow us down so much we ended up missing the cut-off. I tried to just forget where I was for a while and chat to everyone. It turned out Mike and me had a lot of mutual friends in the local running community, and I also learnt that he was a farmer on the other side of Dorset, and so knew what time it was getting light in the mornings. This was a handy bit of knowledge, as it allowed us to plan where we wanted to be by the time the sun came up.

Those massive climbs and descents approaching Lulworth Cove proved to be a real challenge, but when I spied the beam of a headtorch moving very slowly up the cliff on the other side of a valley I tried to get everyone moving to catch whoever it was. Tom was feeling pretty shoddy by now and kept wanting to stop and sit down, but James urged him to keep moving. I kept accidentally shining the beam of my headtorch into James' eyes and am still thankful to him now that he never punched me in the face. When we reached the top of the toughest climb of them all I shouted "You see that, you stupid hill? That's what we're gonna do to all your friends as well." I was just trying to make everyone laugh and keep their spirits up, but I was also having the time of my life and just saying and doing whatever I wanted.

We soon caught up to Ian, who said he'd hit the wall going up the climb and had felt pretty ill. He decided to join us for a while too, and eventually we made it to the car park at Lulworth Cove where, due to some diversions on the cliff path, a minibus was to take us a couple of miles down the road so we could follow the rest of the diversion without adding extra distance overall. I'd been terrified of my legs seizing up during the short minibus ride, and so I practically leapt out when we stopped. I was ready to start running, but Tom fell out of the minibus and started being violently sick by the side of the road. It looked like his race was over for a second year running, and it didn't take long before he told us to go on ahead. Along the next section we were moving well, and Ian's girlfriend would occasionally appear driving in her range rover to offer support. At the next checkpoint we were told we had three hours on the cut-off, which I was delighted with. I couldn't believe how mild a night it was either. I'd put a long-sleeved t-shirt on over my running vest but hadn't needed a coat, hat or gloves at all, and wouldn't end up putting a jacket on until an hour before dawn.

I was really confident about finishing now, and again had a few thoughts of pushing on and letting the others follow if they wanted to, but I was actually really enjoying the company and somehow I knew that I'd be with these guys pretty much until the end. The route beyond here was very undulating, and sometimes there would be a punishing climb, but I was amazed at how good my legs were feeling. The staircase of death wasn't even that bad when it arrived. The talk became more philosophical as the night wore on, just as it always had at raves back in the day. James said about how great a leveller and event like this was, in that none of us had known each other before the race but because we'd had something in common straight away we'd got to know each other pretty well over the past few hours. I couldn't have agreed more, and have always found this to be the way in a number of situations. It would happen at music festivals, it would happen in pubs, it would happen in races. Basically every two people in the world have at least one thing in common, all it really comes down to is whether or not you want to acknowledge it.

It was somewhere not long after the 60 mile point I think that it just started to get light. I'd never run all through the night before, and I'd been told by many that when the sun rises you get a second wind. Seeing as I was already feeling pretty good I was hoping this would be the case. Actually the sun coming up made me think about how I'd not been to bed yet, and I was hoping it wouldn't be too many more hours before I could, even though I was still having an amazing time. I'll never forget when we rounded a corner near Durlston and the sun appeared to be just above the sea, its brilliant orange glow on the water. I was hoping that this meant fantastic times were ahead, and I suppose it also helped to remind me of the enormity of what I had already achieved. A lot of people had told me how tough the ONER was, including some pretty seasoned ultra runners, and things were looking pretty good for me completing it.

When we were crossing Durlston Country Park Mike had told us to carry on ahead. We noticed his absence straight away, as he'd been with us for basically the last 30 plus miles. When we reached the next checkpoint in Swanage Ian's girlfriend asked after him, and I casually glanced up and said "I'm afraid we had to eat him." This was a reworking of a joke I'd got a massive laugh for the first time I'd said it five years previously, and had used at every single opportunity since. It got the same reaction here, and so I'm afraid it will probably be used many more times. As it happened, Mike reached the checkpoint a few minutes after we did. He said we were too quick for him, but he'd just caught up with us so we clearly weren't. We knew now there were no more checkpoints left, but there were still a couple of climbs to negotiate before we got to the final beach section. We pretty much knew we were going to make it, but nothing was guaranteed just yet.

There were a couple of slight disagreements over the navigation on the next section, but in the end we made it to the path that we knew led to the beach. Mike said "So this is it then, I've done an ultra" and couldn't quite believe it. I had my usual mix of being euphoric at what I'd achieved, yet not really wanting it to be over. Ian had been saying for a while he had a pretty nasty blister. He would later show us at the finish, and it looked like a red jelly baby had been glued to his foot. Ouch.

As we hit the final beach section James took off like a rocket. I tried to follow but just didn't have the pace in my legs. After a while though I came across Chris Edmonds, who I had met whilst volunteering at the Thames Path 100 the month before, and who lived locally so had come out to see me. He ran the last mile along the beach with me, along with his two dogs, and said that I was still moving well. I wasn't sure I believed him, but having him to pace me meant I didn't dare stop and walk at any point, which I had definitely felt like doing virtually every step along the sand. It wasn't long before we had to cut in across the beach, and ran straight through some water, which was ridiculously refreshing for my feet. My parents were the other side of the boardwalk that would lead to the finish and for the first time in years I saw them running, trying to get to the finish in time to applaud me in.

Chris said he'd let me go it alone to the finish and would catch up with me in a minute. As I ran along that boardwalk I couldn't quite believe what was happening. I'd done it. I'd actually gone and done it. I'd completed the ONER. So what would I do when I got to the other side? Burst into tears? Scream at the top of my lungs? Collapse in a heap? No, none of those. What I actually did was stop in my tracks, look puzzled and say to the volunteer who was by the dibbing post "Oh wait a minute, I think I've left my car keys in Charmouth", then turn round and start jogging back in the other direction. Then I turned back and went to dib at the finish, dropping my water bottle and shouting at the top of my voice before bending double with my hands on my knees. "It's good to see you've still got a sense of humour" said the volunteer, before Ben came over to congratulate me.

The film crew from the previous day were there and they interviewed me again on camera. When they asked me if I'd be back next year I said "What's that over there?" to Ben and then whispered "No", shaking my head. I quickly added that it was only because I had other plans for next year, and explained how this was definitely one of the best things I'd ever done.

It was actually pretty gutting to have to say goodbye to the people who'd become my new friends over the past few hours. Later that day James would end up having to have a drip in hospital due to severe dehydration. He was fine though, which makes me unashamed to boast that I didn't need hospitalisation, so I must be tougher than an army guy. Or maybe I just managed my hydration better. I was over the moon to hear later on that Tom had battled through his sickness and managed to finish within the cut-off. Rob was there at the finish as well, and had ridden his motorbike all the way to Studland to meet me, which was pretty amazing of him. This was not to mention his giving me a sugary tea just when I needed one and even massaging my muddy calves. He later said he would never massage a bloke's calves again. It was the hair. Fair enough, Rob.

As ever I was massively grateful for my parent's support, and seeing as they'd been awake most of the night I thought it was only fair for us to go home soon after I finished rather than hanging around and basking in the glory for hours, which I felt I wanted to do. I didn't mind leaving though, because I was shattered beyond belief.

I went to running club that week, and my club mate Tanya had got me a chocolate champagne bottle with '80 miles' on it, which was truly awesome of her. A couple of weeks later I ran North Dorset Village Marathon in a new personal best time of 3 hours, 36 minutes, which I was astounded with. I guess it was because I had no expectations for the race and just treated it like a training run, but I felt good from the off and so I kept going with it and ended up running a really good race. I guess the fitness I'd built up during the spring was still with me, but perhaps that marathon took it out of me on top of everything else, because before long I'd start to feel quite fatigued. I was so high on endorphins that I reeled off a massive list of races I would do next within days of finishing the ONER, and I learn a very important lesson. Never make plans whilst high on endorphins. Or at least think them through properly first.

Things starting to unravel

After wondering about going to Australia or to New Zealand for a while, then briefly considering Brazil, I decided I would travel round South Africa. I'd always wanted to go to Africa since watching a documentary about meerkats when I was a young child, then being further inspired by my parents' tales of their trip to Kenya in the 1970s. To get the money together I spent over a year working night shifts in a 24 hour Shell garage. Looking back now, I have no idea how I managed that. I could never do it now. It would be far too depressing. I would often get drunk customers who would give me abuse, and once I got caught in the middle of a huge domestic row, but luckily things calmed down and it was Ok in the end. I suppose at the time I just wanted money to go on my travels again, and would have done pretty much any job as long as it paid. Thoughts of travelling were what kept me going during those nights, but I was also just beginning to find a couple of reasons to stick around. Bob and me, later joined by Sergio, formed a band in late 2005. I say a band, but we also had characters when we played live. The characters, as they had been when Sergio and me had written our sitcom script, were mostly based on real life experiences. One of my favourites, played by Bob, was Old Man Grainger, who had come about because when driving back into town after we'd been to a party on my birthday, but not my birthday party, there was an elderly gentleman driving very slowly up the A358 looking confused. "Oh no, it's Old Man Grainger" said Bob. From that a sordid and debauched old man who was fond of telling people he'd outage the lot of them arose. Another was Turbulence Adams, played by me, who always had advice for people but his brain was weighed down by all the knowledge and so he would always run around shouting "Woooooaahhhh!!!" and occasionally fall to the ground. "He's alright, he's just a bit turbulent. Somebody help him up" Bob would say, and some poor person in the audience would have to help me up and would usually get a piece of advice they may not want.

When I was onstage I was absolutely fearless. I was always sober, unlike Bob and Sergio, but I felt so confident I may as well have had a bottle of vodka. I remember once going out to talk to the audience during a song, sitting on a huge man's lap as I talked into the microphone, then standing up and patting him on the head, saying "Lovely hair, bit too much gel." I would always be doing things like this and no-one seemed to mind. They all just saw it as part of the show. We recorded our songs, but none of us were exactly studio wizards at the time and so they sounded pretty horrendous. Although I couldn't really listen to most of what we did now, and there's no way I could get into the headspace I was in to perform those gigs, because I'm just not that person any more, these were some incredibly fun times. I felt so confident, because I was in a band with my best friends and it didn't matter if people didn't like our music because I was young enough to believe that they just didn't get it and it was their fault. We met so many people from other bands, had some great laughs and we even had some fans. I went to live at Bob's for a couple of weeks in Exmouth, where he was at Uni, and being in the band was pretty much our life for a while. It was almost like being a character again, as I had been when I got wasted, and it meant I didn't have to deal with how empty my life was in other ways.

Also, around this time I discovered something called Myspace. It was the first major social networking that I was aware of, and I guess I was hooked as soon as I got going with it. Like many seem to now I seemed to forget that no matter how much you chat to someone online it's no guarantee that you'll get on in real life, and that 'knowing' someone online isn't quite the same. In the band our best loved song, 'Lightbulbshade', spoke about social networking and the increasing role of computers in daily life. It began with the lines "Everybody's got a Mac these days, I might as well throw my PC away," and later "Do you wanna be my Myspace friend? Isn't everybody on Facebook now?" Anyway, one day late in 2006 somebody commented on one of my photos on Myspace to say that it looked like I was unimpressed with my ukulele. I commented back to assure her I enjoyed playing the ukulele a lot, and then we began messaging each other frequently. She lived near Bath, where I used to go a lot with Bob and Sergio, and so we arranged to meet up a few nights before I was due to go to Africa.

We got on pretty well and agreed to stay in touch while I was away. At the time I wasn't sure if we'd meet up much more, but we'd seemed to really connect when we talked electronically, and we'd had a laugh when we met up in person, so I thought it was probably worth staying in touch. I'd not had a girlfriend for years, partly because after my breakdown I hadn't really wanted to get too close to anyone in case it happened again, partly because I was basically just living for myself for a long time and partly because I just didn't meet anyone I really felt I connected with, apart from once or twice people who already had boyfriends. Anyway, that would have to wait because I was off on my travels again.

I arrived in Cape Town in early January 2007 and felt like I'd won the lottery because I'd escaped the harsh English winter and was somewhere the sun was blazing. On my first full day there though I was wandering around the streets as if I was in Switzerland and I got robbed at knife point. It may seem strange to say it but the guy was actually quite nice about it. He was apologetic and assured me that I wouldn't get hurt as long as I gave him my money. I only had a little bit on me and I gave it to him. It wasn't worth risking my life. He said he wanted more, and asked me to prove I didn't have a cash card on me. I turned out my pockets and he bumped fists with me and ran away.

I was a little shaken up by the encounter, and I wanted to get out of the city as quickly as possible, but I stayed for a few more days and went up Table Mountain. The views from the summit were worth it, even though the magnificence was a little ruined by the internet café and various shops on the mountain top. I never had any more trouble during the rest of my travels. I was a little more vigilant afterwards, but I do think I was in the wrong place at the wrong time and South Africa isn't as dangerous as it's made out to be as long as you're careful.

Once again I could write probably a whole book about my time there, but let's just say the experience was constantly overwhelming. Massively surreal at times. There was one morning I went for a walk in Swaziland up to some nearby mountains. On the plains on the way there were zebras and antelopes. I got to a lake and there were flocks of the most colourful birds I'd ever seen, Carmine Bee-Eaters I think, along with a couple of crocodiles over the far side. I just couldn't believe I was there amongst all this incredible wildlife. Like in Europe it was probably nature that had the biggest impact on me. In the remote coastal village of Bulungula I was so far from any light pollution that the night sky was just a blanket of stars. Everything was accentuated because of the sheer quiet. On the beach the waves were roaring and crashing as they hurled themselves against the shore, and each evening the breeze would get up and throw sand against my skin, which would sting a little. Also on that beach I got chased by a goat one day. I was sat writing in a notebook and I heard bleating off to the right of me. This black goat was walking towards me and seemed to have a lot to say. I got up and started to walk away, quickening my pace but not running, and it followed me until I was off the beach entirely. The night in Africa can be a cacophony of insect sounds. There were grasshoppers the size of my hand, and I quickly became desensitised to them, as I did to the hordes of flying beetles that would appear if you switched a light on at night and the window was open. One of them nearly flew up my nose one night at a hostel in Swellendam, much to the amusement of the guy who worked there.

I went on safari twice; once at Hluhluwe and once at the much bigger Kruger Park. I saw giraffes mock fighting, lions chasing prey, rhinos and buffaloes, and was in a vehicle that was being charged by an elephant. The driver was luckily very skilled at high speed reversing, and said the elephant was only 'mock charging' but it looked pretty real to me. I wasn't scared at the time, it was just exhilarating, but thinking back I'd definitely not want to be driving a vehicle that was being charged by an elephant. Thinking about those encounters now I can't help but be amazed all over again. Coming from England, where we don't really have much in the way of ferocious beasts, at least not in terms of animals, it's just awe inspiring to see what they have in Africa. My comment about the human ferocious beasts in England may seem flippant, but at a hostel in Port St. John's we watched a film about football hooligans one evening and all the South African guys kept saying "Aish!" every time one of the fight scenes took place, and asking if it was really like that. They just couldn't believe that people would fight like that over sport. In Africa there are far bigger fish to fry.

Also in Port St. John's something very significant happened. I took a spectacular tumble from the wagon. I guess this was when I first confirmed to myself that alcohol was a problem for me, after suspecting it years before. I hadn't drunk a drop for five years, and then one evening we went to a local township, where there was a bar. They didn't have any non-alcoholic drinks but I wanted a drink and so I thought "Oh, I'll just have one beer. It'll be fine." That one beer got me quite tipsy. The local kids had been using some of us as climbing frames but not me so far. As soon as I'd had a beer maybe they sensed I'd become more relaxed and so I had one hanging off each outstretched arm and was lifting them like dumb-bells.

Within a few hours I was back at the hostel and knocking back shots of tequila. I was talking nonsense at anyone who would listen and asking everyone for hugs, but I don't think I made too much of an idiot of myself. The next morning I was properly hungover and felt a bit queasy when we all went down to the beach. I was straight back on it the next night though, and barely stopped until some time after I was back in the UK. The trouble was that the booze in South Africa was dirt cheap, and I found plenty of willing accomplices. During a week in the city of Nelspruit I met a guy who had just started drinking again after the recent end of a six year relationship, and he was delighted to have a drinking buddy. For most of the time I was there I did very little but drink and play pool in the evenings, reading and going for the odd walk around in the daytime. I also met a lady from New Zealand who liked a drink or six and the three of us became best friends just for a short time. I only made a real fool of myself one night when I'd thought some Swedish girls were saying I was strange, they were actually talking about someone they knew back home I'd later find out, and I was paranoid that my presence was making things uncomfortable for everyone in the hostel, and so I stumbled outside and fell over, passing out on the grass. An American guy named Evan woke me up and made sure I got to my bed. I told a mosquito that had bit me to go away, something like that anyway, and Evan thought I was talking to him and sighed, but I was too drunk to put him straight.

I was sad to leave Nelspruit, because I was really missing everyone back home, and being there I'd felt like I had some best friends again, even if I was wasted every day. All that remained was five days or so in Johannesburg and then I'd be going home. Everything negative I'd heard about Jo'burg seemed true. No-one seemed to think it was safe to walk around, even in the daytime, and whenever someone would drive us out anywhere we'd see a car crash. I couldn't really be bothered to be there, and was looking forward to going home. I'd had an amazing time in Africa, but if I'm honest I'd found it a bit much not having anyone to share it with. Sergio's wedding would be soon after I got back, and the band had a gig coming up. Speaking of the band, on one of my last days in Africa I saw a lorry that was transporting goods for a popular photocopier manufacturer. This reminded me that just before I'd left on my travels one day I'd had a call at home saying "Hi, is that Dave Urwin?"

"Yes," I'd said.

"Ok....er....that's all I need to know for now."

Let's just say I was a little confused, but then a few days later I

141

had another call from the same person saying that they were a lawyer representing the company whose name was in the name of the band, and that if I didn't want to hear from her again we'd have to change it. I don't think she realised we never made any money from the band, but we just added a couple of x's to the name anyway, just to keep them happy. It wasn't worth the hassle not to.

As well as all the drinking and the isolation I did learn some important things in Africa. These lessons took a long time to properly sink in, and if I'm honest are still doing so now in some ways, but they did leave an impact. Firstly, the people in remote coastal villages like Bulungula, who had almost no material possessions, seemed far more contented with life than well-off businessmen in Johannesburg shopping malls. I overheard a businessman one day speak about a waiter taking ten minutes to bring him his coffee as if it had ruined his life forever. Out in the sticks people would laugh and joke with me and then tell me matter-of-factly how a family member had recently been killed. I've thought a lot about why this discrepancy existed, and the one thing that kept coming back to me was how simple life was for people in the villages in terms of how connected they were to nature and to reality. Of course they had many problems, but they didn't have computers, credit cards, loans or any of the other countless things that complicate our lives and distract us from what's truly important. That businessman was probably so stressed about his coffee because he had a meeting to get to, or had a small window in his fixed timetable to have that coffee break. In the villages people don't rush. They know that things will get done. They know they have to cook, clean, fish and take care of what needs to be done each day but they don't have to fit it all in on top of a stressful job and countless external demands. Like on Fair Isle, their life is all in a small area and it's all right in front of them and is real.

It's easy to paint an idyllic picture of life in these villages, and the fact is that things are very tough. It is hard work to live such a simple life, because food takes a lot of preparation, it mostly has to be grown or caught by the people themselves, there is a lot to do on the land, if they need something they have to make it rather than buy it, and if something goes wrong they have to fix it themselves. If somebody gets ill they can't get to a doctor easily. The list goes on, but they also get to spend every day in the fresh air, the physical work is rewarding, money is not really an issue because there's not much need for it. If a man wants to get married he has to pay the bride's father seven cows, and not everyone owns cows, but there are usually ways round that. Perhaps the man could do some work for the bride's father, or pay him money if he has it. Life is hard work, but everything you need is right there, and if it isn't your existence has taught you to be resourceful enough to find a way round it. Seems wonderful to me, and is something we have really lost sight of. I realise how rich that is coming from me, but I definitely want to slowly implement changes into my life to make it simpler. Living a simple life is not easy in the UK, as you normally need a bit of money behind you, or the help of people who do, in order to do it, but I'm working on it.

I saw signs in Africa that this simple life was under threat. I would look out of the window of a bus and see fields full of brightly painted rondavels, circular thatched huts, but then there would be a gigantic Vodafone logo right in the middle of them. There were also coca-cola logos and clothing brands. I met a villager in Coffee Bay named Kevin. He was a young man, in his early twenties, and he knew who David Beckham was, and seemed to like Western culture. However, his life was very simple, and I could tell when he guided me around that his outdoor lifestyle had given him natural fitness, as he leapt from rock to rock along a river. I wasn't especially fit at this time anyway, but I wasn't especially unfit, and I really struggled to keep up. We got onto the subject somehow of crime and he said there were no thieves in his village, adding that if there were they'd be killed, as if it was the most natural thing in the world. I guess it was for him.

So what really hit home to me in Africa was that often people who had less were far happier than those who seemed to have everything, and it was only when people learnt of a world beyond the villages that they started to want for more. I don't want to be rich, I just want to be in a place where I have enough to get by and can live in a more self-sufficient way. Living most of my life online is just not somewhere I want to be. I always feel happiest when life is simple and I'm surrounded by nature. What is something that always reminds me of this? Running.

Running somebody else's race

We are always told that the most important thing in an ultra is to run our own race. I agree with this completely, but some of the most interesting experiences I've had have been through running somebody else's race. The first of these was when I was sweep runner at the Hestercombe Humdinger, a hilly, scenic 9.5 mile road race organised by Running Forever Taunton, which takes place in late January each year. I had never done this job before, but in 2013 I was training for the ONER and thought it would be a good chance to get some nice, easy miles in one weekend. I'd run the course with some club mates the day before, and considered it a real achievement that I now felt confident enough in my running skills to rock up the next day and keep up with the slowest runner for another 9.5 miles. Considering how unfit I'd once been, this was just ridiculous.

Going by the previous few years' results, I anticipated there being a small group of runners at the back, who I would run along and have a laugh with, but from early on a lone runner dropped off everyone else's pace. "Are you a sweep runner?" she said to me when I stayed with her. I informed her that I was, and she seemed a little disappointed, although I thought she should look on the bright side, because if I wasn't a sweep runner it would have been pretty strange that I was loitering near her.

She would stop to walk occasionally, and kept telling herself that she was going to finish. Here was someone who was definitely running her own race. I was impressed straight away, because I would feel demoralised if the rest of the field ran away from me so soon. Would I have the determination to keep going? Then I realised, I think I probably would, because I'd been where she was. In the 1,500 metres at Sports Day all those years ago the exact same thing had basically happened to me, and I'd kept going all the way to the end even though I finished at least a minute after the second last person did. She kept saying how boring it would be for me having to run with her, but I told her that I'd been where she was and I wasn't racing today, so I was happy to run at whatever pace she did.

As we were nearing half way we were running up the biggest hill on the course as the race leaders were running down it. Race leader Luke Scott came flying down the hill, closely followed by an unidentified runner and Running Forever's resident race winner Phil Burden, and something struck me about those at the very front of the field. None of them looked like they were enjoying themselves. No-one even seemed to notice us going up the hill until club mate Gerry Hogg, who was in fifth place. Often the further down the field you go the more fun people seem to be having. Of course there are exceptions to this rule, such as the Kenyans in Torbay Half Marathon and Robbie Britton in any race he enters ever pretty much, but more often than not the people in the lead are burning with intensity and totally focused on the race. They will be disappointed if they don't win, even if they achieve a time that most of us wouldn't stop celebrating for a month. It made me think of the twitchers dismissing a kingfisher, or the businessman in the shopping centre in Johannesburg irate over his cup of coffee. When you are aiming for the very top it seems that it is easy to forget to appreciate what really matters. In this moment I felt happy not to be at the top of the field, and hoped that I wouldn't get much faster than I already was, because if I did what I lost may negate what I gained.

As the race went on we chatted more and more, and we kept up a good pace running down a hill at mile 7, which Chantelle was proud of. During the next mile she told me she believes that everything happens for a reason, that she felt like I was meant to be there for her that day, and that she had me to thank for finishing. I wanted to assure her that I had not run the race for her, and it had been all her doing to finish, but she really wanted to acknowledge the role I'd played in helping her to finish, and I thought of my not wanting to stop and walk when Chris was pacing me on the beach at the end of the ONER. Perhaps my presence had helped her to keep going in some way, but all of the determination had come from her. I was reminded what determination really was that day.

Chantelle had got into running after having two hip operations, and I found it so inspiring to see someone else's race playing out from start to finish. Someone who had defied the odds to start running, because she wanted to. Someone like me in a way, although I'd never had to have major surgery, I'd just been incredibly unhealthy. When we crossed the line I felt so proud to have been a part of her race, and it reminded me how everyone in the race has a story. I will never get to hear all of them, but seeing as mine is so important in the story of my life I am always interested to hear those of others.

A couple of months later I volunteered at the Thames Path 100. By extreme misfortune for those in the race, but by luck for me, dreadful weather during the previous week had forced race director James Elson to go to a back-up course. Instead of running from Richmond to Oxford along the Thames Path, the participants, or contestants as Boldebort would rather fabulously call them, would run from Richmond to Cookham, and then back to Wraysbury, then back to Cookham, then back to Windsor.... something like that anyway. What it basically meant though was that I would see all of the runners three times, and would get to see the changes in them at different stages in the race, for I would be at the Windsor aid station, which would be at roughly 48 miles, 80 miles and then the finish. As soon as I got there I met Sam Robson for the first time, instantly recognising his sideburns. He had been supposed to be pacing Mimi Anderson, who I had also been looking forward to meeting, but she had dropped out fairly early on. I guess when you've run in some of the places Mimi has it's sometimes hard to drum up much enthusiasm to squelch through 100 miles of mud on the Thames Path in winter. It has to be said, the underfoot conditions were horrendous. People had said it was hard to keep up any kind of rhythm because of the boggy underfoot mess. Sam revealed himself to be a top bloke, and soon he introduced me to a guy who seemed a little bit wasted, spoke like a geezah, kept feeding everyone sweets and dished out the sarcasm in equal measures. I was amazed to learn that this was Robbie Britton, one of the UK's finest ultra runners. He just seemed like such a normal guy, and not the clean-living, eternally wise kind of chap I'd expect such an incredible athlete to be. He reminded me of people I used to hang out with during my days of decadence, in a good way.

As I met more of the volunteers I began to feel massively out of my depth. Phrases like '24 mile swim', 'UK 24-hour championships' and 'The Spine Race' were casually thrown about, and I didn't dare mention anything I had coming up at first, because I thought I'd be laughed out of the tent. However, it turned out that everyone was just as interested in what I was doing as I was in what they were doing. Many of these guys had been at the level I was now at not all that many years ago, and they hadn't forgotten where they came from. Ultra running I have found to be a very humble sport. Perhaps partly because it is still pretty underground, there's not much in the way of prize money or TV coverage and no-one outside of the ultra running community really knows who any of the top guys are, but I think ultra running attracts pretty humble characters. Many of the top runners are often volunteering at races, and give a lot back to the sport in general, always willing to give advice to newcomers who want it.

The race itself was an exciting one, with Dave Ross leading at the 80 mile point. He sauntered into the aid station and asked for his drop bag, a bag in which runners keep spare supplies, that is stashed at an aid station along the way. It had been my job to get these for the runners but I couldn't find his one anywhere. James Elson came into the tent and he couldn't find it either. Understandably he was pretty annoyed, because it reflected badly on him if things didn't run smoothly, and I offered to sort out the drop bags properly because they'd not been arranged in any real order when they were originally placed out. This probably wasn't the fault of whoever did it, because some of them were moved by people looking for theirs during the race no doubt, but it really saved time having a system.

One of the most incredible things I've ever seen during an ultra was when Debbie Martin-Consani, who was in 4th place, went gliding past the aid station with her pacer and husband Marco Consani, who you may remember is a pretty darn nifty runner himself. She had run 80 miles but she and Marco looked like a pair of human gazelles, running with perfect form and in perfect synchronicity. As it was night time and they were outlines in the faint light provided by a lamp on a nearby bridge it was like seeing two ethereal beings floating along. At that point it was the closest thing I believed I'd had to a spiritual experience, although when they arrived back later they revealed themselves to be human by chatting away to the volunteers as if they were just out for a social jog.

Dave Ross unfortunately blew up a little towards the end and was overtaken by six runners before the finish. The race was won by Martin Bacon, whose victory cheer was pretty impressive, and then he sat down for his post-race beer, which I was honoured to open for him, and didn't feel like taking a swig. Interestingly, the second and third place runners were Luke and Richard Ashton. Both were in their first 100 mile race, but they are not related. I would later meet Richard at the South Downs Way 100, and he would tell me that he had some health problems after the race, perhaps due to his internal organs bouncing around so much over the 100 miles. James Adams, who I also met for the first time there, would tell me that it wasn't too uncommon in the longer ultras for runners to urinate blood due to their kidneys bouncing up and down for 24 hours. I've never had anything like that, but it has to be remembered what an undertaking running 100 miles is.

Debbie finished fourth, and then over the next nearly eleven hours I would see many other runners finish their races. It was equally inspiring to see Martin take the win as it was to see Jack Mortassagne, the last runner to finish within the cut-off. They both looked as spent as each other at the finish, and I kept meeting other volunteers who I would find out were top ultra runners all night and into the next day. Drew Sheffield and Claire Shelley I met for the first time there, along with Chris Ette and Gary Dalton, who I have seen at a few races since. What I took most from the experience though was that volunteers are hugely important in ultras, and without them the races would run nowhere near as smoothly. I always make a point of thanking those at the aid stations in every race, and chatting with them, basically trying to make their experience that little bit more enjoyable.

So I'd been a sweep runner, and an aid station volunteer, now it was time to be a pacer. 'Uncle Peter' from my running club, or Peter Hall as he is actually known, was doing the South Downs Way 100 in June 2013 and his original pacer had had to pull out through injury, so I was drafted in. I'd not really run all that much in the month leading up to it, but I figured that my fitness levels had to be pretty good anyway after North Dorset Village Marathon had gone so well, and hopefully for the last 46 miles of 100 Peter wouldn't be too fast anyway, something he reassured me of a lot. For the first half of the race though I got to watch things unfold, and the first major aid station at 22 miles was the last place I saw race leader Robbie Britton, because I would always arrive at subsequent aid stations a few minutes after he'd gone through. Several others I'd met at the Thames Path 100 had fabulous races. Gary Dalton and Chris Edmonds both finished comfortably under 24 hours, Gary under 21. Mark Fox finished in under 20. Sam Robson unfortunately had to drop with a knee injury at mile 22, but showed great spirit in walking 8 miles to the aid station to drop when he couldn't run any further due to the pain. My plan had been to try and sneak Peter in under 24 hours without him realising that's what I was trying to do, and I thought it could happen, but he'd hit a low patch somewhere between miles 22 and 54 and ended up arriving at the Washington aid station, where I would start pacing him, some time after I'd been expecting him.

I'd been up since around 4am after not having slept much the night before, and had been driving from aid station to aid station, where I would be on my feet for a long time, all day. Naturally I was a little tired by the time I started my pacing jaunt. Basically my job was to keep Peter motivated, help him navigate, make sure he remembered to eat and drink and to run at his pace, giving him some company. Early on I kept trying to get him to keep up a decent pace, sometimes forgetting how far he'd already run, and I'd make sure all the applause at the aid stations was directed towards him, rather than me. Being a pacer is all good though, because you are just as entitled to the food and drink at the aid stations as the runner is, and so I had a good feast. I also annoyed a few runners by how upbeat I was, being relatively fresh. "You know there's such a thing as being too upbeat" said one woman. "Ok then," I replied, "I'll tell you what's really going on under the surface, and you'll like that even less." She laughed, and I cried on the inside a little. Not really. Well, maybe a little bit.

I was definitely tired, and actually experienced visual hallucinations during the night and into the next morning. I kept seeing birds on the path up ahead when they weren't there, and sometimes would see headlamps in the distance that would turn out to be glowsticks by the path. I kept Peter going pretty well though because we overtook a fair few people during the night. I would describe to people afterwards the experience of seeing a head torch in the distance and getting closer and closer to it, then passing the runner, who made me think of a merchant with a lamp heading along a trading route in ancient times. I don't know why. As I said, I was tired.

At one point I had to warn Peter of an approaching car as we were about to cross a road. I'm not saying I saved his life, that's not for me to decide, but that was the only moment when the effects of fatigue seemed to be especially strong. I think those 46 miles took a lot more out of me than they did Peter, and I failed a little in my quest to keep things upbeat during the closing miles when I kept saying things like "I am never doing a 100 miler", and

"I must say I'm pretty ruined." For a little while we were with a Swedish guy, at whose race the 100 mile trail world record had been set by Jonas Buud. Normally I would have been fascinated to hear about something like this, but I was pretty worn out and just looking forward to getting finished, and I actually wanted the poor guy to shut up really. Not that I told him that of course.

One of the final aid stations was at a church, and when I sat down I looked up and saw a cross that was letting light in, as it was hollowed out on the wall. I felt a strange sense of calm, and smiled. This moment was soon punctured though when I felt a torrent of pain in my quads. The South Downs are certainly hilly. There is just as much up as there is down, and I was way beyond impressed by Peter's effort. In the final couple of miles the scale of what he'd achieved hit him, and I tried to get him to speed up, but he wasn't having any of it, and quite right too. It was his moment. There was a cycle path that seemed to go on forever leading to the athletics track that we would run round at the finish, but eventually we got there, and as we ran around the track Mimi Anderson could be heard shouting "Well done" as she leapt around waving pink pom-poms at the finish line. I let Peter finish first, his time was around 26 hours, and I was told that I'd only done 46 miles so I should put in a bit more effort really. "Ok, I'll run back to Winchester," I said, "Wanna pace me?" I added, looking at Mimi. She laughed and said no, which was fair enough as she'd done a 290 mile run just a few weeks ago. Claire Shelley seemed to sense that I was a bit worse for wear and sorted out some food for me, then it struck me that I didn't have a clue how I was going to get back to Washington. To cut a long story short, what followed was a taxi ride, two long bus journeys, each with a long wait in between, and then a five mile walk along a busy road with no kerb to where my car was. Then a short nap before a 3 hour drive home. All of this when all I really wanted to do was relax. Who said pacing was easy? Actually to be fair, I've not heard anyone say that.

Needless to say, that whole experience took it out of me a little. I was properly fatigued for weeks afterwards, and this coincided with stresses about money. I thought I was ill and had some blood tests, but it turned out I was just exhausted. The next weekend I went to Bath to run with Tim Lambert, who I had met while volunteering at the North Downs Way 50 in May, and who I was meant to be pacing at the North Downs Way 100 in August. A couple of miles into the run I started feeling sick, and I knew straight away something wasn't right. I didn't manage to get it together, and we cut the run short. It was great to run with Tim, I just wished I had been in better shape, and couldn't help thinking that he was probably cursing his poor choice of pacer. I continued to feel unwell, and mindful of my past I decided it was best not to put any more pressure on myself than I had to, and that it would be unfair on Tim to have to potentially drop out at the last minute, so I told him it was probably best if he found another pacer, and that I thought it was only fair I gave him enough time to do it. He was great about it, and managed to find someone else pretty quickly, such is the way of the ultra running community.

I started to feel better within a couple of months and set a new 10k PB of 43.50ish at the Battle of Sedgemoor 10k in Somerset in August. In September I joined in with a section of a John O' Groats to Land's End run. Stephen Murphy was undertaking the challenge, and I got in touch with him after Mimi Anderson had shared his story on a circular e-mail. It turned out he would be running through Somerset on a day I was free, so I did about 19 miles with him from Bridgwater to Wellington. I learnt two things. Firstly, that running from John o' Groats to Land's End takes a lot of steel. Stephen had gone to hospital earlier in the run and on finding out there was nothing wrong with his heart he'd discharged himself and carried on, even though the doctors wanted him to stay in. Secondly, I don't particularly want to run from John o' Groats to Land's End the traditional way. I don't think I could take running day after day on busy main roads with lots of traffic. It takes a different kind of determination to do something like that.

Stephen carried on and finished his run, which was an awesome achievement, especially considering he was fairly new to the ultra distances, and I went and ran with my club that evening. I ran with the fastest group and pretty much kept up with them, but only because they were taking it fairly easy. They all thought I was crazy for having done 19 miles earlier in the day, my mate James joking that a warm-up run was supposed to be shorter than the actual run. He had a point I guess.

Not long after that I learnt that the first UK 100 miler I'd ever known of, Caesar's Camp Endurance Run, would be holding its final edition in October. I'd always wanted to do it, and I didn't think I was ready for 100 miles yet, I'd not trained anywhere near enough, but if I wanted to do the race I'd have to do it then, so I signed up.

I must admit that when I was fatigued after the South Downs Way 100 I'd become disillusioned with ultras for a while. I didn't know if I was bothered about running 100 miles any more, because now I'd completed something genuinely difficult, the ONER, and my experiences so far had taught me that basically I could achieve anything I really wanted to distance-wise. 100 miles had lost its mystical allure a bit because I'd seen lots of people I knew absolutely smash it, and make it look pretty easy, and so I didn't know if I really wanted to do it any more. Did I need to? The answer was no, I didn't need to. I'd already proved what I'd set out to, which was that I could run ultras if I worked towards it, but did I still want to? I wasn't sure at first, but then I reminded myself how much fun it had been, and reasoned that as long as I approached each race with the intention of enjoying myself then I would. Also, because of the company I'd started to keep I'd forgotten that to most people running 100 miles is still something that seems impossible, it was just that I happened to know a number of people who did it these days that made it seem normal. I figured I'd give Caesar's Camp my best shot. A number of people I knew would be there, so it would be one big party. It didn't really matter how it panned out.

Relapse

The day I got back from Africa I was in for a big surprise. While I'd been away Sergio's engagement had been called off, but he hadn't wanted to tell me until I got back from my travels. Naturally he wasn't in the best place, and he was well up for a drink or ten. I went to the same pub that night with him and his brother Will that I had on the night of my last GCSE exam, and I put my card behind the bar. I'd been used to cheap booze, but when I got the bar bill at the end of the night I said "Ah, that's in pounds isn't it, and not rand?" I meant it. We stayed for a bit of a lock-in, and I'd got the barman and his mates on side by showing them a video from my travels of a Swedish girl I'd met singing a Somerset drinking song I'd taught her. We got a taxi back to Sergio's flat in Taunton and carried on drinking, but somewhere on the way I'd rung the girl I met just before I'd been on my travels and made plans to go and see her later that week. The next morning Sergio and me had a breakfast of Doritos with a selection of dips and had another can of lager each, and then a couple of days later we went for a big night out with Bob. I'd taken to drinking again as if I'd never stopped, but at the time I didn't see it as a problem, because I was still in the travelling mindset. We went to a bar on the high street in Taunton which changed its name every year or so and I can't remember what it was called at the time, but I remember knocking back shots of tequila and talking nonsense at anyone who would listen. At some point Sergio disappeared, then Bob and me were about to walk to his flat to find him when suddenly we came to on the ground. To this day I still don't know for sure what happened to us, but the fact that I was heavily bleeding from above my eyebrow and Bob's front teeth were chipped means someone must have hit us when we weren't looking. I remember a girl stood over us and asked if we were Ok. We said we were and she told us we'd better go. I don't know if we'd been talking to her and upset her boyfriend or what, but we decided to walk to Sergio's and hopefully have a few more drinks.

When we arrived Will was there too, and he seemed shocked by the state of my face. Sergio suggested we go to hospital and get checked out. Will was the only one who hadn't been drinking so he drove us there. We found the whole experience pretty hilarious because we were still so drunk. Sergio was playing the song 'Accident & Emergency' by Patrick Wolf on his phone and we were laughing and singing along. When we got to the hospital the doctors wouldn't see us straight away because of our intoxication, and so we had to sit in the waiting room for hours. Eventually Bob was seen, and within a few minutes a nurse walked out looking irate and holding a pouch of tobacco, some rizlas and a lighter. "Your friend just tried to spark up in the cubicle!" she fumed at us. We looked sheepish, but then as soon as she was out of the room we started cracking up, and I took a bottle of brandy out of Sergio's coat pocket and took a swig, not even trying to be subtle about it. When I think back now it's amazing what a different person I was when drunk. It stopped me from considering anyone else's feelings, and basically turned me into a child in terms of my behaviour. A little while later we started singing 'Film Star' by Suede at great volume, and were told off by a nurse. I didn't know what her problem was, not thinking for a second that someone who was lying ill in a hospital bed might not want to hear about someone who was feeling like a film star propping up the bar, driving in a car, it looks so easy.

Eventually I was seen by nurse Jude, who had to do some stitches on my forehead. I remember it being painful but I didn't want to show it, and I remember nurse Jude was kind, and let us take a picture with her after she'd finished treating me. As we were leaving I said "I think Jude fancies me" to Sergio, loud enough so she would hear, and we heard her laughing in the corridor. I don't think she did really, I just wasn't totally sober yet and thought it would be funny to say. We went for breakfast and the geezah behind the counter commented on my stitches, saying "They don't look too pretty do they?" I said "It's alright mate, the girls love a scar" and he creased up, the look on his face saying "You're alright by me, son!" As we ate he kept shouting to his mate. "Vincent!!!

Vincent!!!" and in doing so earnt himself a place as a character when we played a gig the next week. His name was Bounty Crumbo, and he was all about the ladies. "All you have to do is treat 'em right and buy 'em stuff, that's all you need to know. If it's their birthday get them a jug of water. Not Evian though, it's very expensive. You don't wanna spend that much."

On the Friday of the week I got back Sergio and me went over to Wiltshire to visit the girl I'd arranged to meet up with and her friends. We got hideously drunk again, and she became my girlfriend. I was with her for over a year, even though if we're totally honest we both knew within a month that it would never last. I'd not been in a relationship for a long time and so I wanted to give this one a chance, but it was clear how different we were in ways that mattered. She wanted to go out drinking, and pretty soon I realised for certain that I had a problem with alcohol, so I wanted to stop. She wanted me to stop too, but she didn't want to, because she could control it. This made things difficult, because I had to stay away from anywhere I might be tempted to drink for a while, and although we got on well and had a laugh, and we were attracted to each other, we didn't truly connect. It was inevitable really that there would be problems, and we very nearly split up four months in but neither of us wanted to be alone, so we stayed together. We weren't getting on too well a couple of months later and she cheated on me, but I stayed with her still even though I was never really able to forget what had happened. I was also pretty depressed because for the past few years I'd had plans for my life and now I didn't have a clue what I was going to do next. I knew there was no future in the relationship, but I didn't know what there was a future in.

I thought it was a band. Sergio and me had got together to record a few songs in the spring, and had surprised ourselves by actually writing some half-decent ones. We were both in a place where we were wondering what was next, and so the band came at just the right time. We wrote loads of songs and played some gigs, one of them was even at an all day festival in Manchester. We had people on Myspace telling us we were awesome, including people who made some music we really liked, and we thought maybe we were onto something. Our band name was Verbal Tiger, because one day we used the words 'verbal' and 'tiger' in different sentences on the same day. It was obvious to us.

We recorded the 'Everybody Smokes' EP, and the title track got played on a Bristol radio station, with the DJs saying they really liked it and were looking forward to hearing more from us. The 'John Luscombe' EP followed, named after the author of a book called 'Pig Husbandry' that we found in Sergio's dad's barn. For a while a friend of Sergio's family who worked in advertising said he was going to pay to get 1,000 vinyl copies of our debut album pressed, but it turned out this would be a lot more expensive than he thought. All the same we wrote the song 'Mr Wilson's Pocket', named because if he had pressed the albums we'd be in his pocket. Perhaps my favourite song of ours was called Westonzoyland, after a village in Somerset. The original version was three minutes long and featured a guitar line I wrote that people seemed to really like, and the lyrics were mostly based on an article in a newspaper that Sergio had been reading the day we recorded it. We later recorded a ten minute version, which if I do say so myself was quite good. Another was 'The Transkei Big Five', named after the locals in that area of South Africa's joke about the local wildlife. The big five were sheep, cows etc. rather than elephants, rhinos, buffaloes, lions and leopards. It was an instrumental track with a dulcimer riff, an African drum beat and various vocal samples and sound effects.

Sergio didn't enjoy playing live as much as I did, and it meant he didn't really want to continue the band long term. We stopped in February 2008, just as Sergio was getting together with the awesome lady who is now his wife. At the time I wanted nothing more than to carry it on, especially as my relationship was causing me so much grief, but now I think it's right the band ended when it did. I really don't think I would have enjoyed the band lifestyle, because I remember after we'd played our gig in Manchester I just wanted to get back to where there were fields. The noise and hecticness of the city just wasn't to my liking. I couldn't have faced that day in, day out. I'm so glad we made that music though, and that I got to live that life for a while.

Something else I'm so glad I got to do was when Joe and me attempted the Coast to Coast walk in May 2007. We tried to walk from St.Bee's Head in Cumbria to Robin Hood's Bay in Yorkshire in about two weeks, or ideally less. We'd planned it all before I went away to Africa, and when I got back I couldn't wait to go. At this time I knew nothing about long distance walking, and came woefully under-prepared. My kit was too heavy, I didn't even have a water bottle, so we had to share one, and I hadn't done any proper training. I figured that I walked quite a bit in Africa and so it would probably be Ok. What I ignored was the fact that I'd been drinking heavily for a couple of months, which would have taken a toll on my overall health. So it proved, when we had to abandon our attempt after five days at Kirkby Stephen because I had a knee injury.

We had an amazing time over those five days, walking over a few mountains and through some breath taking scenery, laughing about everything along the way. This was probably the most time we'd ever spent together just the two of us, and we realised how similar we were in a number of ways. Both of us wanted to press on as much as we could with the walk, figuring we might as well while we felt good, and we both had the attitude that we should keep things as humorous as possible because it would seem a whole lot tougher if we didn't. One of the most bizarre experiences I've ever had, and remember the earlier chapter about Glastonbury festival, was on the first evening when a pack of about twenty dogs came charging over the hillside and kept running all the way across the valley until they were out of view. There was no-one near them, they were just a pack of dogs running on their own. We both saw them, so it wasn't a hallucination. Each day we had a different instance of 'dog horror.' I can't remember the others, I think most of them were just some kind of incident involving a dog that we made out to be more frightening than it was, simply because we liked the idea of daily dog horror. Joe and me hadn't always got on well as children, but we always had as adults. It was fantastic to spend that time with him.

I'd been massively disappointed not to have completed the challenge, and had felt like a failure because of it. I wouldn't let my girlfriend see my feet for about a month because they were in such a state from the walk. Nowadays my feet are always in a state because of my running antics, but back then it was something I wasn't really used to. I was also pretty down for some time afterwards, just wishing things had panned out differently. It put a strain on the relationship, similarly when I moved to the area to be closer to her but couldn't find work, and so was just spiralling into debt. Every day I was just stressed about my lack of money, and I must have been a nightmare to be around. Not finding a job also exacerbated my self-loathing, and I just didn't know what I was going to do. I didn't stay in the area long, admitted defeat and moved back once again to my parents' house. It was pointless living anywhere else if I couldn't afford to do it.

Eventually my relationship ended, not mutually, in July 2008. I was devastated, but not surprised. I'd been miserable a lot of the time I'd been in the relationship, firstly because I'd not really known what to do after my travels were over and I had real trouble finding a job, then because of the problems in the relationship but not having enough self-esteem to end it. I wasn't really treated horribly, it was just that we should never have been together in the first place. When it ended I hit the booze again almost straight away, just as I had when my first relationship had ended when I was 16, ten years previously. It was like my life had gone full circle and I may as well have been 16 again. I had no money, I was living with my parents, I couldn't stop drinking and I'd just been dumped.

I was still drinking when my birthday came round in September, and I remember that day well. I drank far too much and made a total idiot of myself, trying to pay for some chips with a ripped note and kicking off when they wouldn't take it, giving a homeless guy a pound and telling him not to spend it on booze, even though I was off my face myself, and walking round the streets at 4am on my own because I was being too noisy in Bob's girlfriend's house when people were trying to sleep. Earlier that night I'd told an ex-girlfriend from years ago's best friend that I thought I loved her just because I was horrifically lonely and wanted to be held. She kissed me but then she said it wasn't a good idea, which she was absolutely right about, and luckily she realised what was going on and was nice about it. The next day I was so ashamed of my behaviour that I wanted to get wrecked again straight away, but I knew that hadn't helped in the past and so instead I just didn't see anyone for a couple of weeks while I got sober.

The last time I drank alcohol I had four pints of Fosters at a gig in Bristol in January 2009. More on that later though, because summer and autumn 2008 were among the darkest times of my life. I just had no clue what I was going to do next. Some days I couldn't stand being around anyone I knew, and so I'd go out to a motorway service station and sit in my car. I didn't want to go to a forest, or anywhere that might actually make me feel better, because I didn't think it would. I thought the silence of nature would just accentuate everything I was feeling and send me over the edge, and so I went somewhere I couldn't hide but where I could be anonymous. There were plenty of distractions, and I would buy magazines and read them from cover to cover. If I couldn't sleep at night I would sometimes drive 10 miles to an all night supermarket, wander round, buy something horrible to eat and then come home, because at least it would use up some time. In the winter I started seeing another girl very briefly but we couldn't have been more different as people and didn't even get on that well, so it ended pretty quickly. My heart wasn't in it. I was just lonely and needed confirmation from someone else that I was worth anything.

Because I'd been on the booze again I'd regressed many years, and was basically for a while trapped in the mindset of my much younger self. I didn't do anything healthy, but there was one thing on the horizon that I had to cling on to. When my relationship had been at its worst I'd signed up to do a trek in Cuba to raise money for Mind. At the time I didn't really know why I'd picked that charity, but then the realisation hit me that it was so close to home. I'd only recently realised that I had a genuine problem when it came to alcohol, even though I'd given up for five years once, and I was starting to finally make sense of what really happened when I had my breakdown. I'd known for years that I got depressed, but I didn't really think I was someone who had depression. When I was younger I was convinced for a while that I was bi-polar, and sometimes I still have moments when I wonder, but I think I'm just someone who was told a lot that he was no good at school and over time started to believe it, then had real trouble shaking that belief.

Late in 2008 I briefly became convinced that I was going to try for a career in conservation. I would save up some money from my current job, then get a volunteer placement on a nature reserve somewhere, learn a lot of useful skills and then get paid work. I liked the idea of it, because I would spend much of the time away from people and out in nature, but then I'd started seeing that girl and got carried away, and would have been prepared to give up on the conservation idea in an instant, so I thought maybe it wasn't for me. That was a lot of my problem though. I didn't really have many skills, because when I was in my late teens I just wanted to get wasted, and then I got ill, then I was totally focussed on saving up money to travel, and then travelling, then I got into a bad relationship and was concentrating on my band. I'd never really had any time to figure out what I could do to make money in the long term, sometimes because I didn't see a future, sometimes because I was too busy being unproductive and sometimes because I thought I'd found a way but it didn't work out.

I did start writing a novel around this time. I'd tried before but had never really got very far with it. Now I had a story I thought was half-decent but I didn't really have much time to write it. I'd had a job in a call centre for a while, and writing a novel really takes time, plus after a stressful day at work I usually just felt like relaxing. Also I'd been reviewing CDs for a local website. It wasn't paid work, but I was hoping it would lead to a paid position somewhere. I definitely loved music at the time, and was on a mission to hear as much of the great music that had ever been made as I could. Sometimes I'd go round to Sergio's, he'd be playing something and I'd be like "What's this?" feeling like it was the most incredible thing I'd ever heard, and would be something I could get totally lost in for weeks. Music was all about escapism. I'd been into it for years, and would get obsessed with a different band every few months. It was a great way of hiding. Of course it was my hobby at the time, and I genuinely liked it, but the amount of money I spent on CDs I may as well have been buying booze, the damage it was doing to my bank balance.

I went to about eleven All Tomorrow's Parties festivals between 2006 and 2012. Each festival is curated by a different band, who headline as well as picking the line-up. At each festival I dressed up in ridiculously colourful costumes, often wearing a Brazil flag, patchwork trousers, zebra sunglasses and an outrageous hat. I would also act hyper all weekend, being the character I thought people wanted me to be, even though I was totally sober at most of them. I did see some fabulous live music. Perhaps a couple of absolute highlights were Vocal Sampling, a group from Cuba who recreated the sounds of all instruments with their mouths, and Tuneyards, a Canadian lady with an incredibly powerful voice, who sampled all her instruments live and then sung over the top. Those two probably got the biggest cheers of any live acts I've ever seen, and they deserved it. I also saw Joanna Newsom a couple of times, which was a major highlight. However, sometimes I would see something that was meant to be genius and just wouldn't get it. There was a jazz saxophonist called Roscoe Mitchell who basically seemed to play a random blur of notes every song. I watched a couple of songs and then said to myself "I don't like this" and walked away. He was meant to be a jazz genius, and I'm sure he is if you like that kind of thing, but I don't.

Anyway I couldn't wait to go to Cuba, and shortly before I left I started walking regularly, noticing a bit of an upturn in my mood as a result. I thought it would be a great chance to give up smoking, because everyone on the walk would clearly be a health freak, and it would hopefully give me a massive boost that would last for some time after I returned. For the record, half of the group smoked like chimneys and so I didn't give up until a couple of months after I got back, but at least I got there in the end. In the week before I left, Cuba was almost literally the only thing I could think about. Everything else could wait for now, it was time to escape once more.

Caesar's Camp 100 mile Endurance Run (October 19th 2013)

Part 1

If you've ever been high up in an aeroplane and looked down on a settlement below you'll have seen that the buildings, roads, parks etc. all kind of blend into one. The closer you get when coming in to land, the more intricacies are revealed. This is the image that comes to me when I look around the runners all bunched together at the start of a race. If you see a photograph of a race start, unless you look closely you'll just see a group of runners, but every one of those runners has a story of how they got to that start line. My favourite thing about ultra distance races is that you will often have time to hear a few of them. Of course you will only get an overview, but I guess I'm fascinated by people, and I guess also I love the fact that everyone on that start line I instantly have something in common with. I feel no inhibitions when talking to anyone during a race, because although we might have different goals within the race, and we might be like chalk and cheese as people in normal circumstances, we are there for the same fundamental purpose. Despite my somewhat solitary nature I have always been searching for a sense of belonging, and rarely have I felt it as much as during a race. Of course you can question what running 100 miles ultimately achieves, even when it's at the top end of the field, and Western States 100 course record holder Ellie Greenwood summed it up well in an e-mail interview I conducted with her by saying "It's a personal achievement for me but in the grand scheme of things I ran from one place to another place in California faster than any woman has before, but how many women have attempted to do that? (not many!) and it's something that only means something to a tiny number of people (ultra runners!) It's cool, it was an amazing day but hey, I didn't do something really amazing like save someone's life or anything like that. I'm super stoked but I keep it in proportion of the grand scheme of life."

That may be so, but I wonder if the story of Ellie's run that day in California sparked something in someone somewhere like tales of others' runs have in me, altering the course of their life in the process. Running has taken the sting out of some of the most intense emotional pain I have ever felt, has gradually given me my confidence and self-esteem back, gave me the motivation to go into counselling and become a more self-aware and consequently more grounded person. Perhaps most importantly, it made me believe again that anything is possible, a belief that has been reinforced further still by other factors that I will speak of later on. In short, running has massively changed my life, and I know it has massively changed other peoples' too. I guess this book is partly the story of how I came to be lining up at the start of the Caesar's Camp Endurance Run 100 miler. Although that day was massively significant in my life I keep it in proportion. Running 100 miles would be a pretty cool thing to be able to say I've done, but it's where else the journey to get there led me that's more important. In essence it took me to a place where I could be Dave Urwin again, the version of myself that I wanted to be, rather than the version of myself I thought other people wanted me to be. Hold that thought.

A turning point

I spotted Rachael from Mind across the room in Heathrow Airport. I could identify her by the Mind t-shirt she was wearing, and she could identify me by the one I was wearing, but she possibly also noticed my furry purple cardigan/hoodie monstrosity, my zebra scarf and the pair of red sunglasses I had on my head. I'd not been off the booze again very long, so didn't have the confidence to turn up somewhere as myself. I had to be in character. She laughed at my costume but seemed to appreciate that I'd made an effort, and as I started to chat to her and the other members of the trekking party I thought I'd made the right decision in coming. I think what happened next is perhaps best told by something I wrote about it just after we'd been. This gives a true indication of where my head was at then, i.e. a fairly scrambled mess but quite a happy scrambled mess, and hopefully gives something of a flavour of my time in Cuba and what it meant on the whole at the time: -

"As you may or may not know, I recently took part in a trek to Cuba for Mind. I thought it would be rude if I didn't say a few words about the whole experience. I mean the magnitude of rudeness of someone who says they will get you a cup of tea and then doesn't, not that of someone who sneaks up behind you when you are enjoying a moment of solitude and bursts a packet of crisps over your head (a huge bag of Doritos, not just a packet of Scampi Fries) then tips an entire bottle of tabasco sauce over the entire mess and tells you to go away without ever apologising for anything, and refuses to pass the salt at dinner while their elbows remain firmly on the table. So yes, what I'm saying is that should I make no attempt to document the journey the world would still be turning and blue would still be blue, but it would be such a waste of all the positive emotion that resulted from my experience should I decide not to turn it into something for everyone to cast their eyes over.

167

I must keep things brief as life in the UK is all about text messages, msn, ringtones, speed dating, electronic top-ups, subway, alcopops, aftershocks, electric razors, gym membership, downloads, designer labels, sponsorship deals, networking, sat nav, digital cameras, video phones, DVDs, mp3s, processed cheese, tuition fees, eating hots dogs in petrol stations, chased away by big Alsatians. Not for us the Cuban pace of life, where dominoes goes up to nine and is the height of intensity. Well let me begin at the beginning, where Mary and Sally proved themselves to be hardcore by sleeping at the airport and I was so terrified of meeting the team that I was literally left with no other option than to rock up in a purple cardigan, pink scarf and sunglasses. I mean, there was literally no other option. Well, no sooner had we begun our attempts to get to know each other than word came over the tannoy that we would not be travelling to Havana that day. Instead we would be spending a day and night in Amsterdam. Well the last time I went to Amsterdam there were lots of shady characters, I took part in 'tag team vomiting' with my mate Jay and I discovered a delicious chocolate milk drink. All in all it was a kind of mixed bag and not one that I was desperate to repeat, but I surmised that I was seven years older and hopefully at least a couple of years wiser than last time I strolled among the canals, leaping out of the way of trams, cyclists and drug dealers. Perhaps this time would be an altogether more wholesome experience. Well actually it appeared that there was a problem with the plane that was meant to be taking us to Amsterdam, and so maybe we weren't going anywhere. Maybe we would be forced to remain at Heathrow and be slowly but oh so surely driven to distraction by the sound of the electronic billboard type thing. It was actually quite catchy if you gave it a chance but even so I was pleased that we would be moving after all. So, to Amsterdam it was, and I was just about getting my head round the idea of a chocolate milk overdose when lo and behold we were stunned on arrival by the news that we would be going to Havana after all. Fantastic.

I don't know to this day if it was my lucky pink scarf, Simoney's prayers or something else altogether, but to Havana we did go. A most delightful morning was spent being wowed by its colourful architecture, myriad of old skool motors, enterprising street artists (one guy's drawing of Rachael looked far more like me) and nicely toasting sunshine. Every sinew of my moral fibre was stretched to breaking point when a young roustabout offered me herbal cigarettes and nasal candy in the market but this was one unfortunate blemish on what was a rather magnificent day. I remember during our trip to Trinidad after the trek that I was a little more inventive with the street traders, dancing away from them or offering my scarf for a reasonable price in return. No-one said 'Si', thankfully. Up until we actually began trekking it was easy to imagine we were simply taking a holiday, and during the second night several of our team did a wonderful job of keeping up the Brits abroad stereotype by almost drinking the bar dry of Mojitos. Emma revealed several of her drunken trademarks during that evening – the Australian accent, the loss of control over her eyes and of course the infamous poker face. Let me explain. During our numerous games of that old classic 'Cheat' she burst into laughter every time she was being dishonest, and my favourite piece of dishonesty was undoubtedly that moment when she cackled "Hahahaha four hahahahaha Jacks" whilst placing down no fewer than twenty cards. Anyway, that night I also managed to remove a rather malicious monkey from my back. Again you may or may not know this, but last year I had my heart trampled on by a herd of buffalo, and then an Albanian scientist named Zork picked up what was left and put it in his smoothie maker, which exploded and sent the liquid hurtling through the air, where it splattered on the pavement and trickled down a drain into a nearby sewer, where it flowed out to sea and was washed up on a distant beach on a faraway island along with some wooden pallets, plastic bottles and pieces of polystyrene. It was then evaporated into the atmosphere before it rained down with great velocity on a road somewhere in South America and became a puddle that a number of kids splashed about in. For twelve minutes.

As much as I tried to hide the above it seems I didn't do such sterling work, as Libby the walk leader, with the eyes of a particularly perceptive Kestrel, noticed something weighing down on my otherwise elated mind. Over a not so insubstantial number of hours she listened as I unburdened myself over the above heartbreak and my subsequent reaffirmation that myself and alcohol just do not mix, and then shared with me some deeply personal experiences of her own. As I talked and listened the realisation struck me that here was someone who had gathered a wealth of experience through numerous travels, both internal and external, as perhaps I have myself, and that we were just two people sharing our wisdom. What's more, here I was thousands of miles from all the disappointments that I had to leave behind. I was still alive, and what's more I was absolutely delighted about it. Everything was going to be cool this Christmas. During the remainder of the journey I shared thoughts and experiences with each and every one of our dream team, and was accepted by them all.

So now to the challenge. Well basically, we stomped up and down mountains, through forests, across rivers and down roads for five euphoric days. We faced a number of hazards, such as Cuban guide Alex's continuous lies ("There are no more hills to go today. Well actually I mean there are no more vertical hills to go today"), the ever-present threat of forest badgers and the cacophony of cockerels followed by Sim's angry protestations, "Up your bum" being the least colourful of the phrases employed in a bid to silence them riotous fowl. I faced another constant threat myself, which was the constant threat of sprocket dispositions. Let me explain. A sprocket disposition is when you say something and you're like "Oh no!" and you eat your own fist. Here is one that could potentially have been catastrophic during the first day, when I was walking backwards down a hill with Sim, as we had worked out that it put less strain on the knees: -

"So how old are you?" I asked.

"Thirty-one" replied Sim.

170

"Oh, right."

"This is when you're meant to say "Thirty-one? But you look so much younger."

"Only if it's true."

It was one of those moments you read about when you hear a voice saying some words and think "Blimey, that was a bit cheeky," before realising with absolute horror that the voice belonged to you. Instinctively I began to run, but after only a couple of steps I heard the welcome sound of laughter, and relief washed over me like Scandinavian rain when I remembered that Sim had a sense of humour. For the record it most definitely is true, and I got my just desserts later that day when I was sat up at the bar at the campsite and Clare said "If Dave was a gentleman he'd give me his seat, but he's not."

One of the most overwhelming things was the level of hospitality we received everywhere we went. Cuba is a communist country, and its people do not get the level of choice in their diet that we have come to take for granted over here in blighty, yet whenever we dropped by anyone's home we were treated to a veritable feast. Next time a Cuban trekking party stomps through your town why not treat them to spaghetti hoops on toast all round, with cheese on top and maybe a few pine nuts thrown in for good measure? Well due to the whole communism thing it's unlikely that you'll see many Cuban trekking parties any time soon, although in time things may change. Whether this is a good or a bad thing remains to be seen. Cuba has a wonderfully relaxed pace of life that could be a great lesson to us over here in our society that is dominated by all the aforementioned things. During our trek I was able to do something that modern life just doesn't allow time for, which is really talking to people. A prime example came when at one point during day three I began to think about one of the reasons I decided to support Mind, which was the suicide of one of my friends seven years ago, and I began to feel sad. I drifted to the back of the group and felt that the best thing to do would just be to remain in my own space for a little while. However, Rachael Taylor seemed to pick up on this and dropped back to chat with me. She asked me questions about my life and about my reasons for being on the trek and after we'd chatted for a while I suddenly realised that I was back in the zone, and skipped up the next hill. This prompted several people to ask me where I get my energy from, and of course it's the same place as I find everything else that gets lost. Down the back of the sofa. However, my energy was tested to the limit the next day when Sally challenged me to run up the first hill of the day, and I ended up racing Emma to the top. Later that day Emma asked me for another race and I began to run but was then glad to find out that she was joking, and I told her as much. Alex took great amusement in this, which led to a conversation in which I found out that Mr Bean is rather famous in Cuba.

I must confess that it was a pretty emotional moment when we crossed the finish line. It was an achievement, there's no doubt about that, but to have shared the experience with such a diverse group, who all added a vital ingredient to the overall soup and worked together like the polar opposite of chalk and cheese; chips and cheese, well let's just say it was exactly what I needed. So what did I bring to the group? Well apart from being the most flamboyantly dressed member of the team I brought along a Cuban flag, which Suzanne Lee had given to me as a Secret Santa present, and carried it on a pole for part of the final day, whilst for much of the trek it was flying proudly from the Russian truck on which our supplies were carried. Other than that, I like to think that at least some of my jokes went down well, and I had the honour of naming the diary 'Steve.' There were also small moments such as the vomit anecdote (although Sim's own vomit anecdote was pretty spectacular) and the story of how Libby retrieved her missing luggage on the final night. I quote directly from Clare: -

"The solving of the mystery of Libby's luggage told with such enthusiasm under the stars on the sand with the sea lapping in the background will always make me smile."

It was thinking about what I had brought to the group that made me more determined than ever to throw caution to the wind at some stage and make a real effort to make a living out of creativity. I have been held back in this respect for most of my adult life by fear of failure, but if such a magnificent collection of individuals could warm to my eccentric ways then what more ammunition do I need against my self-doubt?"

So yes, I had quite a good time in Cuba. I returned to England full of enthusiasm and with a new lease of life. Fairly soon afterwards I found out I was going to be losing my job, because my workplace had lost a contract. I was given some redundancy money, and decided straight away that I would use it as an opportunity to write my novel. There was no-one who depended on me, I didn't have any other ideas, and so I thought I should just go for it. I had no thoughts of getting into another relationship, because after what had happened the year before I just never wanted to feel like that again. If I was to meet someone I knew I'd want to end things at the first sign it might turn sour, and I kind of had it in my head that I wasn't the kind of person who finds that kind of happiness anyway. I thought I was someone who was meant to be alone, because being alone would allow me to write novels.

That's exactly what I did. I wrote, and I started performing stand-up comedy again. First I performed at some open mic nights, and usually seemed to go down pretty well, so I tried to get some actual gigs. I had some success, even doing a very small UK tour at one point. Basically this featured gigs in Weston-Super-Mare, Taunton and York. My gig in York felt like the most exciting thing I'd ever done at the time, and the adrenaline of performing in front of a room of young people who seemed to think I was hilarious meant I didn't need booze. It was around this time that I started to find it hard to be around drunk people. They just annoyed me to be honest. They also acted as a mirror so I could see what I would have been like when I was drinking, and it was pretty uncomfortable viewing. I never wanted to drink again, but

I was still worried that I might be tempted if I was surrounded by people who were wasted. Otherwise how could I relate to them? Therefore I made sure I always had an escape route if I was going anywhere people would be drinking. Several times I just disappeared from parties without saying a word to anyone, because it was easier that way.

As much of a buzz as the comedy gigs were, as with other highs, there still seemed to be a comedown. Two days after my gig in York I was back home living my normal life and felt nearly as miserable as I had the previous summer after my relationship had ended. What I was looking for from this point was some kind of stability. I needed something in my life that was constant, something on which I could rely. I didn't trust anyone enough to try another relationship, not that there would have been anyone in mind then anyway, and financial stability still seemed such a long way off, so what could it be? It was at this point I remembered what I'd done a few months before, and I got in touch with my local Mind organisation. I'd given a talk to some of their volunteers about my breakdown the previous year, and at the time I remember thinking that maybe my experiences would be useful if I volunteered myself. Also, I felt like I'd been living a very selfish life for the best part of the last decade, and so it was time to do something for other people.

Caesar's Camp 100 mile Endurance Run (October 19th 2013)

Part 2

Sleep is a rare delicacy in my current life, and was even more so the night of 18th October 2013. I knew that when I woke up I would be on my way to try and run 100 miles, and just like the night before my birthday or Christmas when I was a young child, the anticipation stopped my brain from switching off. Just like then I managed to eventually grab a few hours and although I felt a little groggy in my dad's car on the way up, as soon as we arrived in the forest clearing of Caesar's Camp and I spotted the notorious Henk Van der Beek strutting around, every last drop of tiredness evaporated away and I was ready to run. Henk had gained a reputation for his no-nonsense attitude. On the race website he speaks of 'cheating sticks', meaning walking poles, and his general disdain for any kind of modern running paraphernalia, and warns potential entrants that they will not receive an ounce of sympathy from him during the race. I'd heard Robbie Britton's story of when he'd been running the 145 mile Grand Union Canal Race (GUCR) and had arrived exhausted at Henk's aid station to be greeted with the words "Right Robbie, you've got two minutes and then you can eff off!" Apparently this was pretty mild. The pre-race conversations on Facebook were littered with warnings to be prepared for Henk's abuse.

I won't lie, I was expecting Henk to be an absolute monster, and to be desperately trying not to make eye contact with him every time I arrived at his aid station. However, the first words he said to me were "Registration's open now, mate" in a very gentle tone. In fact during the entire race he actually proved to be a perfect gentleman. A perfect gentleman with a liking for swear words and who didn't take kindly to sense of humour failures from runners, but a thoroughly pleasant chap. Before the race I also got to chat to a few runners I knew; Dennis 'the machine'

Cartwright, who seems to run a race almost every weekend, had come down to take photographs as he only lived down the road. He spoke of a brutal 10k race that was held in the area, during which there was water to run through that came up to his waist. He is quite a tall chap. He also said that a scene from the James Bond movie Skyfall had been filmed nearby, and it seemed this was a popular location for filming as scenes for the new Man from UNCLE series were being shot here in the days leading up to the race.

I also caught up with Robbie Britton and James Elson, who had both just run awesome races at the 153 mile Spartathlon in Greece. This race holds a certain level of kudos (is that a Greek word?) for many ultra runners, and Robin Harvie based his excellent book 'Why we Run' around his own attempt. Robbie had finished 40th overall, and this was despite, in his own words, 'leaving a 150 kilometre trail of vomit across Greece' after being in 10th place at the 100 kilometre point. Pat Robbins, a fellow British runner who at the time of writing holds the course record for the GUCR, had finished 8th overall after starting more conservatively and working his way up the field, and little did I know until after the race he was volunteering at the main aid station, zapping the barcodes on the runners' numbers as they completed each lap. I called him 'The zapping man' and 'Frank Zappa' at different points without having any idea that he was this incredible runner and incredibly humble and selfless person I'd heard about. He could have finished 7th in Spartathlon but let the guy he'd been running with finish first, and during the first Viking Way Ultra, 147 miles from Hull to somewhere in Leicestershire, he shared the win with Neil Bryant even though Neil had very honestly detailed in his race report how if Pat had wanted to he could have broken ahead and claimed victory. From what I've heard, Pat wouldn't have expected me to know who he was, and that seems to be very common amongst the best ultra runners. At the previous year's Caesar's Camp races some students had been making a film about the run, and afterwards they had gone up to James,

Robbie and Mimi Anderson and asked them if they ran at all. Apparently they replied that they ran a bit, and those students may still have no idea that they asked the woman who has run from Jon O' Groats to Land's End faster than any other woman in history if she ran at all. The thing is though, Mimi Anderson didn't even start running until she was 36, because she 'wanted thinner legs.' She has gone on to break numerous world records and course records and shows no signs of slowing down in her early 50s. Many top ultra runners don't begin showing any great running prowess, but somehow have the right mindset to put in the effort required to go on and achieve amazing feats.

I turned up to Caesar's Camp with the intention of running 100 miles. Starting a diploma in Counselling, having a bit of an ankle injury that needed a rest and not quite having the motivation to fit enough running into my busy life meant that I hadn't trained anywhere as near as much as I'd have liked to, but I tried to convince myself that everything in this book had been training. My life up until that point had sufficiently prepared me to run 100 miles. The look on Robbie's face when I told him my ambitious goal to finish the race before my club mate Tanya started Abingdon marathon the next morning, which would have been under 21 hours, was the look of somebody who'd taken 27 hours to finish the first time he'd attempted the race. He warned me that many people start off too fast and their legs get trashed by the up and down nature of the course, and advised me to walk up the hills, even when I see people shooting off up them at the beginning, because there are plenty of runnable sections to make up time on. Robbie had clearly learnt the same lesson because he came back the year after his first attempt and ran closer to 21 hours. He is gaining a reputation as an excellent coach, and highlights the importance of quality over quantity when it comes to mileage in training, and how vital rest and recovery are in gaining fitness.

Henk's pre-race briefing was something else. When it began with him saying he'd got a sour taste in his mouth because of what he'd had to do to get the race to go ahead this week I knew it was going to be memorable. He was referring to his struggles getting permission from the MOD, who own the land, to hold the race, and this is why 2013 was going to be the last running of Caesar's Camp. I got a real sense from the people who'd been before that this was considered to be a special race, and to finish warranted a certain amount of respect. Not many had come to Caesar's Camp and torn it up. In 2012 Paul Navesey was given a volley of abuse by Henk after his first lap, being told he'd never keep up the pace, but went on to smash the 50 mile course record by running 7.42. To put this effort in perspective, second placed runner Matt Jones finished in 10.26. To give an idea of how tough the course is, Paul has run closer to 6 hours in other 50 mile races and he says that during Caesar's Camp 50 in 2012 he had no issues. In the 100 mile race, Richie Cunningham holds the course record by a huge margin, having run an incredible 18.41 in 2010, which is nearly 2 hours quicker than anyone else has ever managed. I wasn't thinking so much of these runs before the start but of early efforts by Robbie, James and Paul Ali where after promising starts the race turned into a bit of a death march. I was sure this would be more akin to my experience.

"3….2….1….eff off, you lot!" said Henk, and I started fairly near the back of the field, breaking into a gentle trot to begin with. Caesar's Camp is made up of 10 mile loops, and I hoped to get to know the course pretty well by the time it got dark. The midday start meant that this would probably be during or just after the third loop, and so I decided I'd pick up my head torch either at the end of loop 2 or 3, depending on how I was doing. Without meaning to I decided to totally ignore Robbie's advice from the start and ran up the hills, soon catching up with Claire Shelley and Paul Ali. I congratulated Paul on his own recent Spartathlon finish, which had come just a couple of months after the 250 mile Thames Ring race. At the time of writing Paul has finished every race he's ever started, and he's definitely started some tough ones. There was a little bit of drizzle in the air but when we crested the first proper climb the view over the surrounding countryside was stunning. Caesar's camp is a mixture of pine forests, heathland and sandy clearings with a couple of lakes thrown in. At times the Scottish Highlands are brought to mind. In contrast to the previous year though the underfoot conditions, instead of being like a quagmire, were actually pleasant enough, and very reminiscent of the Neroche Forest Herepath, where I do many of my training runs. There was the occasional sharp climb or descent, sometimes there were loose stones and tree roots, but most of the loop was pretty runnable, and having not run for over a week due to fears of aggravating an ankle injury I was like a child let out to play after a whole day spent indoors.

Before long I had caught up with Drew Sheffield, and after a brief catch-up I pulled ahead of him. I kept worrying that I was going too fast, and voiced this concern to Claire, who had caught up with me, and another female runner whose name I never caught, but also mentioned how good I was feeling and that if the pace felt fine maybe I shouldn't slow down. This went against all the advice I'd had pre-race to keep it conservative near the beginning, but I was just having too much fun. I thought I was definitely going too fast when I found myself running alongside Gemma Carter, who ended up finishing 2nd in the 50 mile race. She is also a running coach, and gave me some advice, the slice of which I liked the most was about how if it started to feel tough I should dedicate each loop to somebody who means a lot to me. I'm not sure if I'm going to receive an invoice in the post any day now, but this was just one slice of an entire pie of wisdom she shared with me while I ran with her. I told her quite early on that I may have to let her go soon, and it was nothing personal, because I had to run my own race, but I ended up running probably at least 5 or 6 miles with her and a small group. I hope I get to run with her again in future races, for when she, Thomas Garrod and I were pretending to be aeroplanes running down a hill I knew she was my kind of runner. I am always most inspired by those who remember that it is meant to be fun. Those who seem uninhibited and carefree even when they are running a tough race.

Most of us are out there for the simple reason that we love it. Also that it provides a wonderful oasis of calm from the pressures that go with day to day life. I chatted with another female runner about how this was the most mentally relaxing activity I could imagine, and that it was wonderful to just know I was going to have a number of hours where I didn't have to think about money. She totally agreed, and talked about how running represented freedom for her. I'm not sure I can think of anything that feels so free, and like such a celebration of being alive and appreciating the wonder of nature. We reached the first aid station in decent time. It was manned by Dick Kearn, race director of the CUCR, and his wife Jan along with James Elson to begin with. Others would join throughout the day. I didn't stop for long, and then managed to head off in the wrong direction straight away, unfortunately to be followed by several other runners, but luckily we were called back pretty quickly. The second half of the loop featured some beautifully runnable singletrack trails through the woods, alternating with some epic climbs and then the final mile or so was a gentle downhill on an expansive path followed by a sharper downhill on a muddier path and then a sharp incline followed by a steep descent into camp.

I remember absolutely bombing down one of the descents near the end of loop one, and the looks on Henk and Robbie's faces when I approached the aid station said "Why are you treating your first 100 miler like a trail marathon?" I was on an absolute mission at this point, and Henk even had to yell at me because I nearly ran right through without having the barcode on my number zapped. I scoffed a couple of jelly babies, put a fun-sized mars bar in my pocket and set off on my way, running for a couple of miles with Thomas and the mystery female runner. Conversation flowed, the miles seemed to pass quickly, the rain had stopped, the scenery was wonderful, but wait a minute I didn't remember that barn on the right hand side of the path. We'd taken a wrong turning. Oops.

It's amazing what effect that error had. After I'd been having the time of my life, the five or ten minutes lost getting back on the right track made some negativity creep into my brain, which had the instant effect of making my legs feel heavier. I had to let Gemma, Thomas and the others go, and plodded along at my own increasingly slow pace. When I reached the half way aid station I perked up a little, saying to Dick "Now that's an ultra beard. One I can only dream of." He laughed, and told me that I could have one if I just left my beard for a few months as that's what he did. James told me my pacing seemed sensible. Little did he know about my aeroplane antics, and running alongside folks I knew would be going faster than I should be. I actually felt pretty good for a mile or so after leaving the aid station but then the cramp started. At first I was almost able to run it off, but then on one of the bigger climbs it started really burning. I told a runner I was with at the time that I needed some electrolytes when I got back to camp, and he kindly gave me one of his s-caps, but when I got to the descents heading towards camp I knew that I had a battle on my hands. Of course I'd cramped up in races before, but never to the extent that I had to sit down by the side of the trail and stretch, which is what was happening now. People passed me and asked if I was Ok. I told them I was fine and just had a touch of cramp, but at that point I was actually thinking that if I couldn't shake this off my race would be over. There'd be no way I could carry on like this for 80-plus miles. I'd be here until Thursday.

Changes

In summer 2009 two things happened that would become a huge part of my life over the next few years. Firstly, I began volunteering for Mind in Taunton and West Somerset. My enthusiasm probably frightened the manager Andy Pritchard. Anything he had going on I would volunteer for, much of it was talking to the public about mental health, which I did at events in various town centres around the county. It amazed me how some people would come up and talk to me, a total stranger, about incredibly personal experiences. I heard some stories that made me think my own life had been a picnic, but I was reminded that I shouldn't think like that. Life is not a competition to see who has it the toughest, and if something makes you feel stressed or unhappy then it is important to you, so it should be important to others. As men we are encouraged to keep it together and not express feelings, which many believe is a factor in suicides being more common amongst men than women. I have found in my own life that if difficult situations or feelings are not dealt with then it can have a pressure cooker effect on the brain, which can lead to what happened on the A303 on that afternoon in February 2003, and the months of hardship that followed. I am certain that thousands of people suffer in silence, and if I would give one piece of advice to anyone it would be to not do this. The Samaritans are always on the end of the phone, 24 hours a day 365 days a year, and I have personally found that talking to someone has really taken the edge off some feelings that could have torn me apart if I hadn't dealt with them at the time. If you don't want to speak to a stranger then think about who you trust most in the world and ask if you can speak to them. Even though it may be difficult to listen I can bet that person would rather this then to see you fall apart because you had no-one to talk to.

Also in summer 2009 I met Boldebort, who became my best friend when we signed up to do the Three Peaks Challenge together for Mind. During our training we realised how much we share a silly sense of humour, and several of our training walks are still some of the best adventures I've ever been on. No-one makes me laugh as much as she does. The first day we met up, which we'd decided to because we had a mutual friend, and because she wanted to borrow a colourful hoodie I had that she'd seen in a photo, there were several strange incidents that probably should have warned us what we were in for. For instance, a lady walked past where we were sitting carrying a pigeon. We laughed about it and were viciously told off, being told it had a broken wing. How often does something like that happen? Over the years the number of ridiculous things we've laughed about I've long ago lost count of. I've always found that laughter is one of the best ways of coping with life, and I think pretty much every day on which I've seen Boldebort we've laughed pretty hard about at least one thing.

My mate Bob I've laughed with for years too, and in 2009 we started making short comedy videos together in our spare time. We've not done any for a long time now, but it's absolutely true that one of them was once played to a classroom of children in France. It was called '90s/00s Internet Redux' and featured a character who lived his life on the internet. "Another great day on facebook," he said near the beginning, before the internet went away and forced him to see what life was like in the 90s, when people actually did real things. He had dialogue with a character from the 90s, who was just as bemused with the modern era as he was with the one before. It was designed to show how much life has changed in such a short period of time and to poke fun at the digital age. A teacher in France, who was a fan of our videos, decided his class could learn some valuable lessons from it. He was probably right. It frightens me to think that children nowadays are growing up never having known a time without the internet. I guess it's the same with every generation, things are changing all the time, but I became pretty obsessed with social media when it first arrived, and probably lost a lot of touch with reality. Getting involved with Mind started to bring me back to what was important, which is proper, meaningful, face to face contact. I'm not sure it's a coincidence that depression and anxiety are on the increase nowadays when a lot of modern life is not lived in the real world.

Something else that changed around this time was that I began to realise I didn't enjoy performing onstage as much as I used to. I was writing and performing poetry around 2010, the best of which was probably a poem called 'Love is a Barely Seaworthy Fishing Boat'. You probably don't have to be a genius to work out what it was about, and it included lines like "That's why whenever someone tells you that they love you they might as well be telling you that one day they will destroy you," and "Not one of those unkind sparrows would look my heart in the eye, which it didn't even have because it was a heart." Another poem I wrote by taking some of the lyrics I'd written for Verbal Tiger songs and putting them through a couple of different translators on Google and then back into English. I don't remember many of the words, but one line was "Glass broken remains on the pavement, to sweep it may remain within." That sounded pretty deep to me at the time, even though I couldn't tell you what it might mean. I joked to the audience that when writing the poem in this way I'd stumbled across the discovery that Jim Morrison of the Doors had written all of his lyrics in this way. Mind you, in his day there was no internet, so he had to use foreign language dictionaries. Very time consuming. I seemed to find the concept of people using antiquated methods to do things that were on a parallel with what people did now hilarious, as in my comedy sets there had been a bit about the Grand Old Duke of York having to do tapestries of his conquests rather than taking polaroids. Very time consuming. However, that's a different story.

When I performed nowadays the nerves beforehand were so intense that the momentary high I got if it went well just didn't seem worth it. A few times I would cancel scheduled performances because I just didn't feel in the right zone to perform. Perhaps I just didn't need to any more, and so I didn't want to.

After Cuba I'd really got into walking again, and whilst writing my novel I'd go for a walk most days, sometimes for a number of hours. I noticed the improvement it led to when it came to my stress levels, my overall mood and my level of focus. At the same time Mind received some funding to start an ecotherapy project, which would allow people experiencing mental distress to get involved in conservation or gardening work, reconnecting with nature. Project manager David Topham said at the time, "Ecotherapy is just a posh way of saying get outdoors and do something physical and you'll feel better. It's not complicated, but it's very effective." I went out with the group on a couple of occasions and it was amazing how relaxed and uninhibited everyone seemed, when the same people had seemed a little tense and awkward when in the office waiting to go to the nature reserve beforehand. I would later interview a participant in the sessions as part of my role as PR Champion for the project, who would tell me that the ecotherapy he'd found to be so much more effective than any group therapy sessions he'd had to be a part of in hospital. He talked of how the institutionalised atmosphere in the hospitals made everyone naturally defensive and withdrawn, whereas in the relaxing surroundings of nature he felt like he could talk to anyone about anything.

In 2011 I played a big part in organising 'Walk on the Wild Side', a walking challenge that would raise funds needed for the project. From having taken part in several challenges for Mind I was able to blag my way through the organisation process, even though I'd not done it before, and I was walk leader. Six of us completed a 30 mile walk on the Quantocks, with about another 10 joining us half way round for a 15 mile walk. We were lucky with fantastic weather on the day, and the event was highly praised by everyone who took part. Similar observations were made to those on the Cuba trek, with people speaking about the amazing camaraderie between all these people who'd never met, because we had a common purpose. Between us we raised around £5,000, which was enough to make up a shortfall in funding for the project. This remains probably my finest hour being involved with Mind, after my volunteer role turned into a paid job as PR/Fundraising Co-Ordinator.

Another was when after a tip-off from Andy I got in touch with Laura Gallagher, a trampoline gymnast from Somerset who had previously won the under 19 World Championships and then developed an anxiety illness that meant she was frightened to get on the trampoline some days. She had now learned to manage it well, and was hoping to represent the UK in the upcoming Olympics. We felt like her story could be inspiring for people, and so I found an e-mail address for her and got in touch. A couple of weeks later we filmed an interview, conducted by my new volunteer Ellie King on her first day in the role, in which Laura talked very honestly and eloquently about her experiences. The video is still on Youtube, and having watched it again I am reminded what a brilliant job Ellie did. If I hadn't known, I would have thought she had done hundreds of interviews. The three of us appeared on BBC radio Somerset a few months later and during the interview Laura let slip that I was running a marathon soon, which prompted the interviewer to ask which was more difficult. I truthfully said that I'd rather try and run 100 miles than attempt some of the moves Laura does on the trampoline.

I did the Three Peaks Challenge twice, which involves climbing Ben Nevis, Scafell Pike and Snowdon all within 24 hours. Just stating a fact here, but nowadays I'd find it pretty easy in comparison to some of the challenges I've taken on. At the time it seemed like the most ridiculous challenge I could imagine. The first time was in September 2009, the day after my 28th birthday. Simoney from the Cuba trek was there, and it was great to be on another challenge with her, but unfortunately she wounded a thumb in a trekking pole accident on Ben Nevis, and after valiantly carrying on with her arm in a sling, this perhaps meant she overcompensated and wounded her knees, which meant she couldn't join us on Snowdon. Also regarding trekking poles, at one point when we were travelling between Ben Nevis and Scafell Pike Khanya, one of the participants, said "What do you think of these poles then? I'm not sure I like them," I instantly said "Don't be so xenophobic", which probably got as big a laugh as anything did during one of my stand-up gigs. This is the joke I am most proud of from my life so far, and a couple of ultra runners have stolen it for their blogs without crediting me, but that's where it came from. So there. We completed the challenge, and I'd not wanted it to end, so I was delighted when Boldebort asked me to take part in it with her the next year.

The second time we didn't complete the challenge, but we had a fabulous time. Boldebort didn't enjoy Scafell Pike in the dark very much, but we had a great laugh on the whole, in fact we enjoyed it so much that we decided to do another challenge as soon after as possible, which was the Charmouth to Weymouth walk I believe I mentioned earlier. This was just before I properly got into running, which became something I could always rely on to take the edge off things.

Being involved with Mind was a great stabilising influence in my life, but sometimes I still got very depressed. My novel hadn't been published, which had led to a massive crisis of confidence, and my work for Mind was incredibly rewarding but in money terms I wasn't making enough to move out of my parents' place, which was something I felt I had to do. I had no idea how I would ever make much money, and although I don't care about being rich it can't be denied that having enough just to be comfortable is something that makes life far easier. When I'm out running it's a great opportunity to stop thinking about money for a while. Thinking about money made me thoroughly miserable around these times. Life seemed to be a series of towering highs and crashing lows. I was ploughing so much of my energy into my work with Mind that I often forgot to look after myself, and so when a low point came I would be pretty exhausted and wouldn't have the energy to deal with it. Sometimes I would find getting out of bed the hardest thing to do. It can't be denied that beds feel more comfortable in the morning, but some days I just wanted to stay there and hide from the world.

It must have been around November 2011 that I began to realise I wasn't doing what I started being involved with Mind to do, which was to provide one-to-one support for people, and to use my own experiences to help others. My job was becoming more about the fundraising side of things, and I realised that even though I had the occasional great success it wasn't where my real strength was, or where I wanted to be. I couldn't believe that yet another thing I'd tried to do for a living was going to fail, because that's how I saw it, but I was also struck with a massive dose of inspiration as to what I would do next.

Caesar's Camp 100 mile Endurance Run (October 19th 2013)

Part 3

So there I was trying to stretch out my calves and hamstrings by the side of the path, and all I could think about was how I didn't want Henk to see me like this because he'd give me both barrels. Of every verbal sawn-off shotgun in Hampshire. I didn't want my parents to see me like this because they'd worry. I didn't want any other runners to see me like this because it would look a whole lot worse than it was, and they might waste valuable time checking if I was Ok. Basically I knew in myself that I just needed to get back to camp and get some electrolytes in my water, have something salty to eat and then walk it out and I'd be just fine to carry on. I was able to draw on my previous experiences to know that this would pass, but should it really be happening this early? I'd started cramping not too long after half-marathon distance. That wasn't normal. It had to be due to the up and down nature of the course, and the fact that I'd run a little harder on the first loop than I'd trained for. I'd been running as if I was at the same level of fitness as during the ONER, when actually I'd only done about four or five proper runs over the past month. Nothing could change that now. I just had to make the best of what I had anyway and hope it was somehow enough.

The thought of dropping this early didn't even cross my mind. The thought of running 20 miles on this kind of terrain would be terrifying to the vast majority of people, and in the grand scheme of this race I'd only just finished getting warmed up. Ten years ago the thought of what I'd just done would have made me completely unsurprised that I was cramping like this. In fact I would have thought it would be impossible to take another step. Things were different now. After stretching out though I managed to stagger my way back into camp, and I think everyone could tell I'd felt that loop. "Give us your best crazy face, Dave"

189

said Robbie as I approached. "Er....yeah, that's pretty crazy" he said at the face I made in response, which was probably a very polite version of what he was thinking. I can't have looked well. I got my barcode zapped and then told my parents I needed electrolytes, so my dad opened the boot of his car. I dropped half an electrolyte tablet into my water bottle and then devoured some rice pudding and crisps at the aid station. There was no disguising the fact that I felt pretty shoddy at this point, and I picked up my head torch because I was fairly sure it would be dark by the time I got back to camp again. Something that was becoming apparent to me at this point was that I hadn't panicked, even when the cramps were so bad I could barely walk. I'd been here before and come out the other side, and from that I drew some comfort. On the other hand, the prospect of my race being over didn't seem to cause any anxiety. I didn't think much about why this was at the time, but I guess I'd only known I was doing this race for six weeks or so, and so I'd had almost no time to build it up in my mind as a major event. I wanted to finish, and would do everything I could to make it happen, but I hadn't spent much time visualising crossing the finish line, or planning how I would celebrate if it happened. There wasn't much fanfare attached to this race, like there had been to others previously.

Heading out of camp, I started power hiking up the first climb. Henk was waiting in a tree at the top of the hill, and said "Come on, ladies. Get a move on" as myself and another runner I'd caught up with passed. "Lovely day" I responded, and he agreed before leaping out of the tree and charging down the hill, discarding lots of loose stones in the process. It was starting to get pretty gloomy by now, and I actually remember very little about this third loop except that I told James Elson how shoddy my last one had felt and he seemed a little concerned. I suppose he was right to be, because 75 miles is quite a long way to go if you're firing on all cylinders, never mind if you're feeling a bit shoddy. I did start to feel better during the loop though because I remember running a bit with Benjamin Kissel, who was running the fifty, and pulling away from him when approaching the half-way aid station. In fact by the time I got back round to camp again I was positively buzzing, and practically sprinted across to the aid station there. My parents knew I was fine because I was dancing to the Leonard Cohen song that was playing out of the speakers as my dad repeatedly asked me "What do you need?" I grabbed some shot blocks from him and had a few bits and pieces from the table before quickly heading out for loop four.

As I started jogging off up the first climb I made a noise that was something between an owl's hoot and a battle cry. It seemed to help, because I kept up a reasonable pace for the first couple of miles and soon caught up again to Drew Sheffield, who was having a few issues but couldn't quite put his finger on what they were. Something was out of balance, that's all he could figure out for now. We continued to leapfrog each other all the way to the half way aid station, not literally of course, it's a running term, although this has just reminded me of something that happened during lap one. I'd been running in the slipstream of a group of three, one of them had asked me if I wanted to pass and I said "No, I'm all good thanks, mate. If I do want to I'll just do a flip over this guy's shoulders." I was very much joking. Something that really struck me was how warm a night it was. I'd not had to put another layer on over my Running Forever vest yet, and I wouldn't at any point apart from for a minute or so after leaving an aid station and when it rained a little once or twice. It was also nearly a full moon. I later said this to Henk, and added that he must be really annoyed about it. "Yeah, it is kind of disappointing" he laughed, but he got his wish in the end when it started chucking it down just after dawn.

Just before the half way aid station I ran past a group of cub scouts who were out with their leaders for a night's camping. "How far have you gone?" asked one of them. "Thirty-five miles," I replied, "I've got another sixty-five to go." I heard a few gasps, before one of the cubs said "You're mad." I'm pretty used to being told that now, including because of my ultra running antics. I guess it could

191

be considered not the sanest thing to be out running through the woods all night when you could be snuggled up at home with a hot chocolate and a good book. If it hadn't been such a balmy autumn night I would probably have thought the latter option was more appealing, at least I'm honest, but right at that moment I couldn't have been happier to be where I was. I'd overcome the cramp issues that threatened to end my race when it had barely begun and I was in that magical place where I felt like I could just keep plodding along forever. The endorphin high was off the scale, and I hadn't even needed to eat any of the fly agaric mushrooms that were dotted around the course. There had been plenty of jokes about these earlier. I'd been talking about how difficult the race would be if we were tripping on top of it.

"Not that you'd know" said Gemma.

"Of course," I replied, "I lived a very sheltered life in my early 20s, honestly." The mystery female runner had said "Somehow I don't believe that" and I'd jokingly accused her of being judgemental because I had a beard. For about twelve minutes.

Drew came into the aid station a couple of minutes after I did, just before I was about to leave, and when he sat down he had the look of a man who was contemplating how far he had to go and not being entirely thrilled at the prospect. I tried to keep his spirits up by telling him we would finish together and noting the many similarities between us; that we were both 32, we both had dark hair and we were both rather handsome. I was being tongue in cheek regarding myself, but I've read several blogs that have mentioned Drew's facial exquisiteness. People also frequently comment on his granite calves, which are quite likely honed from running in the mountains, but at that moment in time he seemed to be feeling a little defeated. It happens to us all at times, even to the very best. The previous month Mimi Anderson had had to pull out of her double Spartathlon attempt due to ketosis, an acute condition that can develop during epic runs if you don't eat enough in the process. And yes, you did read that right. Mimi was attempting to run the Spartathlon and then turn round after a short rest and run back to the start again. She does things like that; earlier this same year she had become the first person to complete the double GUCR. She doesn't do it to make the rest of us look bad, she does it because she's running out of traditional challenges and so has to invent new ones. It is surely only a matter of time before she attempts Jon o' Groats to Land's End and then back again.

During the second half of this loop I was really starting to feel incredible, and was even running up some of the climbs at a steady pace. I was now beginning to recognise plenty from each loop. There were several sections that began with a cattle grid, there were a couple of style type things to climb over and a single gate, whilst I began to recognise certain sections from the underfoot feel. There was a nice, flat runnable section that started with some soft, liquidy mud, and then there was another flat section where an incline began half way through but it was only a tiny incline onto another flat forest path. There was a fallen log across part of the path, just after which was a lovely gentle downhill section. There was a nightmare of a climb that emerged onto a sweeping vista, admittedly not quite as sweeping in the dark. Actually though I found the course easier to follow at night because of the plentiful glow sticks that had helpfully been placed in trees around the place.

When I completed loop four Henk asked me how I was feeling and I said I was absolutely fantastic, which wasn't a lie. My mum said I looked bright as a button, and that's exactly how I felt. I scoffed a few potato wedges and some more rice pudding, had a cup of coke and decided to head out again straight away while I was still feeling good. One more loop and I'd be half way. One more loop and I'd still have half to go. At this thought my mind began to waver.

The Core Conditions

I'm kind of suspicious when it comes to psychological theories. Although a lot of them make sense to me when I learn about them, and I can apply many of them to my own life, I'm uncomfortable with the idea that people's behaviour can be explained with science. This seems far too black and white a way of looking at things. However, there is one that makes sense to me more than any other, and that's Carl Rogers' theory of the Core Conditions. He argued that what we as human beings need to experience in order to flourish is empathy, congruence and unconditional positive regard. If I can break this down, empathy is when someone makes the effort to understand something from our viewpoint, or trying to walk in our shoes, imagining how something would make us feel from our own perspective. Congruence is basically being real, and being honest in a gentle way. Unconditional Positive Regard is realising that there are reasons behind our actions, even those that don't paint us in a good light. If you think about it, surely this is what we would hope for from our loved ones, or what a Christian would expect from God. When I think about it, experiencing these things from someone always puts me at ease, even when I am in real torment, and these are the qualities I hope I display as a person to people I care about. Of course it is difficult, probably impossible, to display these three things at all times because we are all human, and we are fallible, but what if somebody had a window of time set aside in which I could be prepared to display these things to them?

Counselling seemed like the natural career path for me as soon as I had been through it myself in 2011. My first counsellor, Josephine, was a runner. As soon as I knew this I saw her differently straight away. At first I'd found it hard to open up too much, and had felt like I was the clueless, broken one and she was there to try and fix me, but in time I realised that this isn't how counselling works. Counselling is about the counsellor and client developing trust and then working together to work through the client's difficulties, with the counsellor acting as a guide and keeping the focus. I thought of the Three Peaks Challenge, when we had guides who would take us up the mountains and make sure we didn't get lost, but we'd still have to walk every step ourselves. As soon as I knew Josephine was a runner I was able to relate to her a lot better, because I knew there was an interest we shared. At the time she was counselling me I thought I'd only be able to find common ground with people who shared my interests. It can't be denied that this helps, but what really matters is what you're like as a person. I think this very point is argued at the end of the film 'High Fidelity', but that's not where I got the idea from.

The best work I did with Josephine was to learn to think more rationally, and to realise when my self-doubts were due to those I had as a child. At the time though I thought as soon as the counselling started to work that would mean I was cured, and I'd not get depressed any more. The truth is that life is an ever-shifting emotional landscape, if you want to look at it like that, which it helps me to, and happiness and sadness are not constant states. No matter how well things are going in life there will always be something that tests us, and no matter how badly things are going there will always be something to remind us that things aren't hopeless. This is what I worked on more with my second counsellor, Hannah, who I saw between July 2012 and September 2013. I knew I needed further counselling before I saw her, as I still felt woefully inadequate as a person, but I never thought I'd be there for over a year. When I first got to a place I thought the process could end I think I tried to sabotage it by panicking about my money situation. I was training to be a counsellor myself, and to have the time to do this I had to quit my job at Mind and find something that would be less taxing on the brain. I managed to find a job proofreading from home. It did my head in, and paid barely enough to cover my petrol and food costs for each month, but it fit around my college studies. I didn't fancy my chances of finding any other job that would, and couldn't think of anything I could do self-employed that would be a reliable source of income, so I was stuck with it. I'd been in and out of my overdraft, and of substantial credit card bills, ever since I'd started Uni, and in summer 2013 things were looking pretty dire. Eventually I realised that things weren't going to get any better if I just panicked about it the whole time, and so it was just a matter of letting go and realising that if things got too bad I'd just have to quit my course and get a full-time job doing something else. It would be horrendous, but I'd have no other choice, and knowing that would mean that somehow I'd find a way to not let it happen.

I think the most significant work I did with Hannah was realising that I can't control the way other people are with me, but I can control how I respond. I learnt to accept that I can't change things about people, but can learn to accept things as part of who people are. Also, she told me of the quicksand analogy. This is basically that if someone was sinking in some quicksand you could either jump into the quicksand with them and sink as well, or you could offer them a branch to hold onto from the outside and try and help them out. Which would be more helpful? This means that if someone is feeling sad, or stressed, rather than taking on that feeling yourself and feeling like you can't be happy if someone else isn't, you should try and offer that person understanding without mirroring their feelings of despair. I had begun to feel like it was my responsibility to make sure people close to me were happy, and if they weren't I'd feel like I'd failed, but I can see now how massively unrealistic this was. Nowadays if someone is sad I recognise it as their feeling, and will try and offer any support I can without feeling like it's my responsibility to solve all of their problems. Basically I put so much pressure on myself that all of my relationships for a start had been doomed to fail. I'd felt like if I wasn't the best boyfriend ever then people would grow tired of me pretty quickly, and rather than being myself, which is what someone would first have wanted to be with me for, I would constantly worry about whether I was a good boyfriend and as a result would be a pretty bad one because I'd always be inhibited and tense.

I would also look at people of my age who were married, had children and had well-paid jobs. I had none of these things, so I thought I must be a massive failure. I think many people do this to an extent, but there were times when I literally couldn't stop thinking about it from the time I woke up in the morning to when I went to bed at night. I'd failed at life. I was no good. Everyone else was far better. However, in time, and after many sessions talking to Hannah, I started to genuinely believe that it was pointless to compare myself to other people, because I wasn't them. My life had gone differently to theirs, and even if my life hadn't turned out exactly how I wanted so far, what really mattered was what I did from now on.

My money worries weren't the only thing that sabotaged the counselling process. In January 2013 a friend of mine, Dan, who I'd known through Mind, was hit by a bus and fell into a coma, never regaining consciousness and dying in hospital. He was 34, which was only a couple of years older than I was, and it shook me to the core. I just couldn't understand how someone could disappear from this world in an instant, and I guess some feelings resurfaced from when John had died all those years ago. I couldn't get my head round it, and it made me want to retreat from everything, so that's basically what I did. I used my poor money situation as an excuse to take on loads of overtime at work, and did a lot of running, using the excuse that I had to train for the ONER. The running was definitely something I wanted to be doing, and something I enjoyed, but once again I was escaping. I guess I thought that maybe I could be taken away any moment, and so perhaps it was best if I wasn't too close to anyone. I got into my own space, and that's where I wanted to stay. Luckily this only lasted a few months, rather than years, and pretty much as soon as I'd done the ONER I felt like myself again. For the first time in years I was actually getting a pretty good understanding of who I was, what I genuinely enjoyed doing and what was important to me. The most significant realisation came in a session with Hannah when she asked me what I wanted to be and I said "I just want to be Dave." I didn't want to be a top ultra runner, I didn't want to be outrageously rich, I didn't want to be the best at anything, I just wanted to be myself, and I was coming to realise that this is what other people wanted me to be too. If anyone liked me it was because of who I was, and so why did I need to try and be anyone else? If someone's respect was worth having I wouldn't have to earn it by trying to be who they wanted me to be. I wonder how differently my life would have turned out if I'd taken this approach when I was 16. How would my first girlfriend have reacted if I'd told her I was a birder? Would I have been less popular at college if I hadn't been wasted all the time? Would I ever have got into running? As with my conundrum on Countdown, I will never know. All I do know is how my life did turn out.

I want to be a counsellor partly because I'm fascinated by peoples' stories, and I believe that everyone has a book in them, the story just has to be told in the right way. If I'd chosen different parts of my life to write about this could have been a book about how I sat around listening to music or reading books. I could have written more detail about the boring jobs I had, and tried to make that interesting. The point is that everyone has been through something. Some people could write incredible books at the age of 20, others may have to wait until they're a lot older, but life is fascinating and everyone has something that is worth writing about, whether they believe it or not. What is interesting to one person may not be to somebody else, but no matter who you are there will be people who are interested in what you have to say. That's why there are different sections in bookshops. That's why people have different social groups.

Going through the counselling process allowed me to look at my life and make sense of it all, realising that there were reasons why things had turned out the way they had, and many of them were beyond my control. It's so easy to look at someone's life and think that you would have done things differently, but it's all about context. It's hard not to judge people, but the only way you can truly know what you would do in any given situation is if you find yourself in it. I am taken back to the Georgian man speaking of his philosophy on life in that hostel in Switzerland, and then how everyone had the same reaction to the stunning view out of the window of the art gallery. We all have similarities as people, but our experiences are all different and that is why different people behave and react in different ways. Both of my counsellors gave me a space in which I could explore why I made the choices I did in life, and why my life has turned out the way it has. I'd be truly honoured to be able to do this for other people, and I aim to complete my counselling training in the next couple of years. However, going through counselling also reminded me that I had a story to tell. The novel I wrote was basically a lot of this story before I got into running, but with different characters and a few details changed. I'm glad the novel didn't get published, because my life got a whole lot more interesting after I wrote it, and I realised that I didn't need to hide behind a character, because that's what I'd been doing most of my life. It was time just to be David James Urwin, which is what I was meant to be doing all along.

Caesar's Camp 100 mile Endurance Run (October 19th 2013)

Part 4

As I began my fifth loop I started to feel some undeniable differences from how I'd felt during ultras before. Instead of a desperate man with everything to prove, who would finish at any cost, I felt like someone who had been there before and would be there again and could just enjoy the experience for what it was, regardless of what happened. A number of people had reassured me over the years that when you get older this is what life's like. It probably isn't for everyone, but I can see already how I feel like I have less to prove in my early 30s than I did in my early 20s, and my priorities are beginning to change. As I made my way around that loop I began to forget a little about the race situation and just thought about how nice it was to be out in nature. How much I enjoyed being away from a computer screen and surrounded by trees, feeling the mild evening breeze on my face and the ever present endorphin rush as I kept putting one foot in front of the other. I took a swig of my electrolyte infused water and smiled to myself, saying "That's nice" out loud as if I was an old man sipping a nice cup of tea.

A couple of times during this loop I did start to hurt a little, and I thought about how I didn't have to be here. I was here because I chose to be, and I could be sleeping in a warm, comfortable bed. I could be sitting on the sofa with Boldebort laughing about nonsense. It was good to be out here, and I hoped I would always want to be a runner, but I guess the biggest realisation for me out there in the woods was that although I wanted to be here I didn't need to be. I could survive without it. If I didn't complete this race I would get another chance to run 100 miles if I wanted to. Maybe I could train better next time, and psyche myself up more, and perhaps pick a slightly less challenging course. My lack of training was beginning to find me out, and I could probably guts it out for a twenty-six, twenty-seven hour finish but did I really want to? Would I consider myself a failure if I didn't?

I started to think about how my parents hadn't been to sleep yet. They were out here waiting for me to get round each loop because they loved me and they wanted to see me doing things that made me happy. The guys at the aid stations greeted me warmly every time I came in, even Henk most of the time, because they thought I was a nice guy. I'd told Boldebort I would hopefully be back in time so we could hang out on Sunday evening. I was lucky enough to have a best friend with a sense of humour as strange as mine, who wanted to spend time with me because I was David James Urwin, no other reason. If I didn't finish until 3pm the next day I might not be able to see her. I wanted to see her. I wanted my parents to be able to go to bed. I knew there were people from my running club and elsewhere who wanted me to do well and to complete the race, but at the same time I knew that they wouldn't want me to do it if I was going to break myself in the attempt.

I thought about dropping when I got to 50 miles, because then I would still be considered a 50 mile finisher, but then I thought about how this was the last Caesar's Camp and how I'd signed up to do the 100, and so I owed it to myself and to everyone who cared about me to at least give it a go. After all, this was only one day. At the 50 mile point my dad asked me if I was still feeling good, and I said that I felt like I had run 50 miles but I still felt pretty Ok. I tried not to spend long in the aid station, and then headed out for loop six.

During this loop a gradual deterioration began. My legs got sorer, my eyelids got heavier, I got a bit more weary and managed to wee on my shorts a bit by accident.....sorry. When I got to the half way aid station a guy asked me if I needed anything and I said some new legs would be good.

"Anyone got any new legs?" he said.

"We've got some knackered old ones" laughed Dick from somewhere in the gazebo.

"You're welcome to those if you want them" said Henk, emerging from the shadows.

"Already got some of those I'm afraid" I replied, but then tucked into some cheese and prepared to get on my way.

From this point onwards the rest of the loop was a bit of a death march. Gemma and Claire had warned me earlier not to let any negativity creep in, and at the time I'd been sure it wouldn't, but now the thought of dropping was becoming more and more appealing and as a result my body tried to convince me it had nothing left. A couple of miles from camp I bumped into Benjamin again, who had taken a wrong turn on his fourth loop and added on a good few extra miles. He was just coming to the end of loop five and was feeling pretty dreadful himself, so we decided to trudge back to camp together. I'd hoped to have completed seven loops by this stage and I was just about to finish my sixth. If I had been on target maybe something would have changed in my mindset and I would have found something extra, but Benjamin could tell I was close to dropping. We chatted about life, and he told me how at one point he'd been working 40 hours a week and then focusing for another 40 hours a week on his acting, unpaid, so nowadays he'd instead found a job with a sports adventure company so he could do something he enjoyed and get paid for it. I told him I was training to be a counsellor, and he said he'd thought about doing this, just as Gemma had earlier. I think it's a pretty common path among ultra runners, because I guess some of the same qualities are necessary for both. A lot of patience, strength of character, open mindedness and determination sure help. It was fabulous to have the company, and I think if I hadn't bumped into him I'd quite likely have dropped after loop six.

We jogged into camp together and my parents could tell straight away I was in a fairly major low patch. My mum looked worried, and I tried to pretend I was feeling better than I was whilst still admitting I was tired. I asked for a sugary tea and took a seat for a few minutes to drink it. Henk appeared once again. "You look like something from a film," he said, "Not a good film." He was probably right.

My parents asked me what I was going to do and I said I would head out for another loop but if I felt worse than I did now afterwards I might have to reassess things. They hugged me and then I started jogging out of camp, knowing straight away that this would probably be the last time I did. Not in a fatal way. I didn't feel remotely disappointed in myself. I, who couldn't even walk a hundred metres from my front door in 2003 without having a crippling panic attack, had run 60 miles on a brutal course having done little in the way of training, and knew that if I really wanted to I could run further. The thing is I didn't really want to. If I did then maybe I'd have a glorious finish and sneak in just under the overall cut-off, but what would the ultimate difference be if I did or I didn't? The point is that I had started the race, and given it my best shot. With that in mind I decided I'd keep going until it felt preposterous to carry on, and fairly soon my prayers were answered when my ankle injury flared up and every few steps it became more painful. I knew at this point by carrying on I would be doing myself more damage, and would be unable to run for longer afterwards. With over 35 miles still to go I knew that to carry on would not just be inadvisable, it would be irresponsible. There would be other chances to run 100 miles. The fact that I was Ok with that told me I had done something far more important. I had finally been able to accept myself. I didn't need to complete any more feats of endurance running to prove that I was a worthy human being. I didn't need to run another step to do that. All I needed to do was to try every day to be a better person, knowing that I won't always succeed, but to help the people I care about, to look after myself so I can better look after others, to not waste this wonderful gift of life that has been given to me. Life doesn't always seem like a wonderful gift. Sometimes it feels pretty shoddy, even when you have a positive outlook, but being in it is what matters. I had faced every one of the past 1,000 plus days sober, had done things that seemed impossible to me, and had shared some of the best times imaginable with some truly wonderful people. I could easily have never had that chance, but I did, and I still do. I am one lucky person.

As I reached the half-way aid station for the final time I said to James "Is there anyone still out there on the course after me in the 100? My ankle injury's flared up and I'm thinking of dropping"

"Will what I'm about to say change your mind?" he asked.

"Say it and I'll tell you" I replied, and Dick laughed.

"It'll take me a couple of minutes to check" said James.

I let him check. Jan offered me a hot dog and I said if I dropped I'd have one. Another guy who'd just decided to was sat in a chair next to James looking utterly spent, but he smiled. It only took a couple of minutes before I decided this race was over. I was relieved. I sat in a chair and accepted the offer of a hot dog with mustard, and it tasted incredible. I tried to make everyone laugh, telling James that it had worked out well for him that I'd dropped because now my first 100 mile finish could still be at one of his races. I then told him that this meant it was his fault, because his presence at the aid station had made me guilty this wouldn't be the case, and so I would sue Centurion Running. I'm not going to really.

I also commented on how the playlist at this aid station, mostly rap, made a change from that at Henk's, where there was mostly country music. This is something I love about ultras, how each aid station has its own vibe, and this is because of the people. Everyone brings their own personality, and I hope that I've done the same when I've volunteered in the past. For now though it was time for James to give us a lift back to camp. When I got there the lovely aid station volunteers told me they'd found it inspiring how I'd headed out for another loop considering the state I was in, and Henk was thoroughly pleasant about it, shaking my hand. Peter and Lynn from my club, who'd been doing the 30 miler and were between loops 2 and 3, were there and I chatted with them for a while, wishing them luck on their final loop, during which heavy rain was due. I was even less bothered not to be continuing. Don't get me wrong, I like to challenge myself, but on this occasion I knew that I was underprepared for the task in hand, and once my injury flared up I knew that common sense must prevail. The prospect of food, drink and sleep seemed far better than that of mud, pain and exhaustion this time.

I will give running 100 miles another go. I am proud that I completed 65 on that course. It is now five days since the race and I haven't run again yet, but am looking forward to starting again after a few weeks' enforced rest. A vegan would probably say at this point that it's more about the journey than the destination. That's basically what I would be trying to say if I was to offer some kind of conclusion. To have run 100 miles would be, will be, an awesome achievement, but what matters more is to pretend to be an aeroplane running down hills, to slow down and talk to the other runners as I pass them, to show my appreciation to those who have given up their time to man the aid stations, to take in every sight and sound along the way, to make people laugh, to run harder if I feel good, to slow it down if I don't, and most importantly of all to always remember the second and third scenarios in the introduction of this book and how lucky I am to be starting these races in the first place. Life can take us to some pretty dark places but where there is hope there is always a way out. No matter what Henk may try and tell you.

The future

The strange thing about the future is that by the time you read this a lot of what is the future now will be the past. With that in mind, when I talk about the future now I am talking about the future from early November 2013. Let's just clarify that.

Good. Ok, so by now you know that I attempted to run 100 miles and didn't manage it. Will I try again? Well at the time of writing I'm signed up to run Thames Path 100 2014, one of four fabulous races organised throughout the year by James Elson's Centurion Running, which those who've been paying attention will know I volunteered at in 2013. After facing horrendous weather conditions two years running, James decided to move 2014's race to early May, when hopefully things will be considerably less boggy underfoot, and the night section will be a lot shorter. I'd be pretty confident of finishing this race if I was uninjured going into it, and if my mind was on the job on race day. At 2013's race James told me that he believed the ONER was about the same difficulty level as Thames Path 100, because although the latter is 20 miles longer it's considerably flatter and is mostly on very true paths. Well, at least if the weather's been dry leading up to the race.

I hope to run Thames Path 100 as many awesome folks I've met in the course of my ultra running shenanigans will be there. Dave Ross, Gemma Carter, Dennis 'The Machine' Cartwright and a number of others will be on the starting line, and of course James Elson, Robbie Britton, Drew Sheffield, Claire Shelley and many others will be at the aid stations. Basically once you've done a few ultramarathons they're just social occasions with plenty of eating, plenty of banter, plenty of laughs and admittedly quite a bit of running, but if you didn't like running you wouldn't be doing ultras in the first place now would you?

I'm not sure which other races are on the horizon. I'd maybe like to do Seaview 17 again next year, and perhaps something in the Autumn, but I think I'd like to only do a few races a year so it's a real event when I take part in one, and is something to look forward to for months. There are so many great races out there, and so little time, but I've noticed that when I try and pack a lot of races in they just don't feel as special and I don't enjoy them as much. Also I don't have so much time just to enjoy running for what it is, because I'm spending much of the time recovering. I'm tempted to stop racing altogether, because I don't feel like I have much left to prove. I've run times at every distance up to marathon that I should be proud of, and I've completed something properly difficult in the ONER. I do enjoy racing, but I don't feel like it's something I need to do any more.

Admittedly there are a few that I'd love to have a go at one day. UTMB, a 100 miler round Mont Blanc through France, Switzerland and Italy and then back into France looks like a massive party. What puts me off is how hard it is to get in, with there being a lottery system, and then even if you do it might not go ahead in full. Twice in recent years it's had to be changed to a 62 mile race due to atrocious weather. I wouldn't mind having a crack at the Grand Union Canal Race, which is a 145 mile jaunt from Birmingham to London along canal paths. Call me strange but I actually love running by canals. I think they have their own kind of beauty, and I could imagine myself running alongside them for hours on end, which I'd have to. It takes quite a while to run 145 miles, especially if you're not one of the quickest out there, and so it would be an epic old adventure. There are a few other races around the world that kind of appeal, but I don't feel the same burning desire to take part in them as I did a couple of years back. I think back then I felt like I had everything to prove, to myself as much as anyone else, but now I don't. Rather than chasing after these incredible experiences I'd like to work on making my day to day life more to my liking. Instead of having the massive highs and then the epic comedowns I'd like to have a solid base of contentment. Then I can go after those highs again if I want to.

So what would contentment be for me? Well I think I've hinted that I'd like to live a more natural life. I'd like to have a place of my own close to nature where I can grow things, build stuff, keep animals perhaps and basically live more like people did before all this modern technology cropped up. I realise the irony of saying that when I'm sitting typing this book on a computer. Believe me, if I had the time to type this all out on an ancient typewriter I'd love to, but modern life doesn't allow for such luxuries, especially when you're struggling to make money. How I make my money at the moment is all connected to computers, but I'm hoping that by doing this now I'll be in a position to make money away from the computer before too long, or at least spend far less time on one. At the time of writing there's a café for sale on the Isles of Scilly. I've been there on holiday the past two years with Boldebort her son, to the Isles of Scilly, not just to this café, and we've been saying how wonderful it would be to live there.

As you may remember, there was a chance I could have grown up on the Isles of Scilly. If I had I think I would have appreciated it in a very different way to how I would if I lived there now. If my family had moved there when I was 2 I'd never really have known what it was like to live somewhere with a faster pace of life, and so it just would have been normal to me. Now it would pretty much be paradise. I wouldn't have to drive anywhere on the Isles of Scilly, wouldn't have to worry about crime because there basically isn't any, would be able to get wonderful food from the numerous farm shops and hopefully grow plenty of my own, spend every day by the sea, run every morning around the cliff paths and on the beaches if I wanted to. In short, life would be simple and everything would be in one place. Here on the mainland I can easily feel out of sorts because everything is scattered around, I have to drive pretty much everywhere if I want to visit friends or get to shops and things feel inherently complicated most of the time. I think back to those villages in Africa, and why people seemed so contented there. Of course living in a small place could have its drawbacks. It would be hard to be anonymous there, and I do like a bit of my own space sometimes, and in order to live there a reliable source of income would be needed as it's not cheap.

The second time we went we agreed that as soon as we got there it was like we'd never been away. It felt like home. When I got back after the second time I knew more than ever what kind of life I wanted to live. I wanted to be more connected to nature, more connected with people, more connected with reality. To do this I knew I had to make money, but how? In trying to figure this out I found way more than I'd bargained for.

We got back from the Isles of Scilly just before my 32nd birthday. I mentioned earlier about how I wish all of the money I'd ever spent on intoxication could be paid into my bank account tomorrow. On return from the Isles of Scilly I began to wonder what I could do to make it happen. I had a problem because my proofreading job, even if I did 20 hours' overtime per week if it was available, wouldn't pay incredibly well, but I didn't have the time anyway because I was soon to resume my counselling training, and I didn't fancy being a hermit. If I was going to do this I'd have to be more inventive, more pro-active.

I'd not prayed much in my life, but seeing as I'd spent years trying to make enough money just to not have to spend half my life thinking about money, and not had any success, I figured I needed all the help I could get. I'd thought for a long time about how wonderful it would be if I could believe that as long as I had faith then everything would work out Ok. How was I meant to have faith though when I doubted myself so much? The day before my birthday I prayed for a sign to show if it was worth me even trying. I didn't really think much more about it, and then that evening I created a page on 'Go Fund Me', where people could make a small donation to help me buy the café on the Isles of Scilly. I was absolutely serious about it, but only wanted the odd pound here and there towards it, and was going to do everything I could to try and raise money myself. I had a huge CD and vinyl collection. Most of my CDs I never listened to because

I just didn't have the time. I didn't have turntables any more, so the vinyl weren't needed. Also I was looking to live a life more grounded in reality, and so I didn't feel like my Garmin or I-pod were in keeping with this. They could be sold. Then I had a running backpack I'd bought the previous year but hadn't got on with. Any unexpected money that came my way I would put towards the fund. In itself it wouldn't be enough, but hopefully if I made a bit of money selling things I could turn it into more money somehow. I could be inventive.

I had a great birthday, eating ice-cream and playing crazy golf in Ilfracombe, then throughout the week I was noticing that things were going pretty well on the fundraising front. People had gone out of their way to help, seeming inspired by the story, e-bay sales seemed like they were going to really pay off and I was being bombarded with new ideas all the time. Then when I was driving home a few days later in the afternoon I saw the end of the rainbow. I mean literally. There's no other way to describe it. The biggest rainbow I'd ever seen was arcing across the sky and right down onto the road in front of me. For a good minute or two I could see the end of the rainbow shimmering on the road right in front of my car. There's no way I can do it justice with words, but I just couldn't believe what I was seeing. I'd heard that you can have acid flashbacks years after taking the drug, where you start to feel like you're tripping again for a little while, but that's not how I felt at all. I'd never felt more sober. I don't believe that what I saw was a hallucination. There would probably be some reasonable scientific explanation, but then I kept finding further pieces of the jigsaw.

The previous year I'd read a book called 'From Alcohol to Atacama' by Billy Isherwood. It's Billy's true story of how he became an alcoholic after a horrific childhood, but then eventually ran a multi-stage desert marathon in Chile and found faith in God. The first time I picked it up I read about a page, then got distracted and forgot about it, reading a number of other books in between. However, something drew me back to it and I found it to be one of the best things I've read. It's told in Billy's real, no nonsense northern voice, if you hear him speak it sounds exactly the same as he writes, and tells a story I could identify with many things from. Towards the end of his book he speaks of how he decided to see what this whole God thing was all about after speaking to a Christian whilst in hospital. After being very sceptical about the whole thing he was absolutely overwhelmed by the feelings that were stirred up in him. He started to believe in God, and started to pray, and describes how amazing things have kept happening in his life since. I got in contact with Billy to ask if I could speak to him about my experiences, and his. He e-mailed me his phone number and we arranged a date and time that would suit both of us to have a chat. Just before I pressed the 'call' button I saw rainbows on the screen of my phone. This was just getting too odd, but I didn't feel scared or confused. Billy was on his way to the North York Moors when I called, and his fiancée Bridget had to pull the car over into a layby as he thought he might lose reception if they kept going. He'd said that he was a busy man but he always had time to talk about God, because he owed him so much. I'd decided to speak to Billy because he'd discovered his faith relatively late in life, as I wondered if I was beginning to, and he seemed like someone who believed in God but was still incredibly down to earth, and had a silly sense of humour. Equally as importantly though, I didn't know him. If I was going to tell people I knew well then I wanted to be pretty sure first.

I talked to Billy about what I'd experienced, and he told me some stories that it reminded him of from his own life. He then spoke to me about how he believed that if I accepted God into my life amazing things would happen, because that's what had happened for him as soon as he had found his faith. He also assured me that if I was to accept God into my life it wouldn't mean I had to radically change who I was, because he could tell I had a good heart. I could still have fun, I could still be myself, I would just have to be more conscious of the way I was living my life. I am still very early on in my understanding of what this could mean, but a couple of things I've picked up on straight away are that many things that have not brought me happiness in life are things that are not in line with what I believe God's will to be. I believe that God would want me to live a life closer to nature, to use my negative experiences and turn them into something positive, and not to waste my time on earth despairing of things I can't change, but to make the best of every day. I won't lie, it is very difficult to do this when faced with the drudgery of daily life, the bleak English winters, the fact that there aren't enough hours in the day to do what is expected of us as part of this society, but what is important is to try. I'm planning to make a list for 2014 of 100 things I can do to live a more positive life, and will keep referring back to it. Also, it is not up to us as human beings to judge each other. By that I don't mean that no-one should go to prison for murder, or even that it's easy not to have prejudices, because I believe that pretty much everyone does. One of my own is that whenever I am introduced to a stereotypical bloke I fear that we'll have nothing to talk about, but often I've found this not to be the case if I try.

At the end of our conversation Billy said a prayer that he'd felt inspired to, saying to God that he felt he was trying to stir up my spirit and asking that he continued to do whatever it was he was doing. I had already started to agree with Billy about what was happening. I knew that people had been praying for me to find a connection with God, and I could either believe that the world was full of incredible coincidences or that their prayers were starting to be answered. I thought back to May, when there had been prayers for me to have a safe journey to a race I was volunteering at in Surrey. I'd been unsure about what to do; Robbie Britton had offered me his sofa to sleep on the night before and I was originally going to take him up on this, but I was totally exhausted and so decided to drive up early in the morning after a few hours' sleep. When I'd nearly got to where the aid station was that I'd be volunteering at the oil light came on in my car. I pulled into a garage and bought some oil, but then the bonnet just wouldn't open. Normally it had opened just fine. I wasn't going anywhere without putting more oil in, and so after trying everything to get the bonnet open, well just the usual method actually but many times, I called the AA. As was bound to happen, the mechanic got the bonnet to open straight away and looked at me like I was an idiot. I assured him that it wasn't working before, but it was lucky he was there because it turned out what I'd thought a little while ago was a very minor oil leak was actually the cylinder head gasket packing in. The mechanic said that he'd have to take me to a garage because he couldn't let me drive off with the car like it was.

On the way I educated him about ultra running. Like most people when I tell them about it he couldn't believe that people run 50 or 100 miles in one day. I laughed on the inside as just a couple of years back I couldn't believe it when I read about it. Now it was beginning to seem almost normal. He gave me a lift to the aid station as well, but my car was no more. The fact that I'd managed to complete my journey safely could be seen as a massive coincidence; it was an incredible bit of luck that the oil light had come on just before a garage rather than miles from one, but was it a coincidence? After I'd talked to Billy I began to have my own prayers answered quite frequently. One day I'd seen somebody I knew in a state of unmanageable stress and upset, which they'd ordinarily be in all day if they were in at all. I had to get to work, but I prayed and asked God to help them find a way to cope with the day. Literally twenty minutes later I got an e-mail from that person apologising for the state they'd been in and describing rationally why they'd been able to calm down.

Also, I asked God to help me find some clarity as to how I should go about overcoming my money troubles and getting to a point where I can live my life in the way I feel I should. Almost straight away the idea of writing and self-publishing a book came to me. I'd been starting to make half-decent money from e-bay sales,

I'm not talking thousands, but enough to cover the initial costs and order some copies of the book to sell. After doing some basic calculations I figured out that I wouldn't actually need to sell that many copies of the book in order to be able to make more than I was making from my proofreading job. I started to write and it just poured out of me, because I knew the story back to front. It was the story of my own life, how I'd developed addictions as a means of coping with unmanageable levels of self-doubt, how the fall out had been spectacular but I'd found a way to start living my life again, then after some truly testing times I'd started to find stabilising influences. Then I'd proved to myself I could do something that I'd thought was impossible, and through counselling I'd begun to make sense of the past and begin to let it go. The trouble was that my life didn't just pause while I was writing. New things were happening all the time, and so if I was going to write my story I had to do it quickly. Time wasn't something I had, and I briefly made the decision to quit my proofreading job, but then something told me it wasn't a good idea and that I'd just have to somehow find the time around it, and my college studies, and my life. I literally have no idea how I did it, but probably about six weeks after I started writing the book I've almost finished it. I just crowbarred any time I could, and found levels of focus and determination that I discovered I had through ultra running, but struggled to find in daily life.

Another massively significant change was that I felt able to end my counselling. I'd been going for over a year, and as I previously mentioned I'd got to the point once or twice before where I felt maybe I was ready to leave, but had done something to sabotage the process. The fact is that there's never an optimal time to leave counselling. There will never be a time in life when everything is absolutely perfect, but the time to leave is when you have got to a point where you feel able to cope with the stresses that will inevitably come in life without the counsellor's help. I felt I'd reached that point, because I'd learnt enough about myself through the sessions and through my training to be able to look after myself. I also knew that if I felt I needed counselling again at any point I could come back. It wouldn't make me a failure, just human. What's more, I now believed in a higher power. Ultra running is what taught me that to get through anything in life you have to have faith, but my answered prayers are what absolutely confirmed it. I promised at the beginning of this book that I wasn't going to tell you what to do if you're not Ok, and I'm going to keep that promise. I've told you what I've experienced that made me believe in God, but if you've not lived through it then it's just words, and if you've had similar experiences then you'll get it. If you haven't you may think it's nonsense, you may not.

Anyway, as long ago as 2008 I knew I wanted to turn the darker experiences of my life into something positive. I did this through my work for Mind, but I knew that one day I wanted to write a book. Now the time is right, as through the unexpected ultra running adventures I had I found something around which to anchor the story. Some of the experiences I've talked about you may think I'd just want to forget, but I've learnt over the years that pretending something isn't there just because it's painful means it hurts twice as much when I'm forced to deal with it later on. Nowadays I want to deal with painful experiences and difficulties head on, and I want to recognise what I went through as being absolutely crucial to where I am now. I also believe that experiencing the absolute horrors I did in my youth made me better able to experience pure joy. If I have one hope for this book, admittedly other than it making me some kind of living, it's that someone will read it who has been through something similar and it will help them to feel that they are not alone, or to start to make sense of what they've been through. Failing that, I hope people laugh at some of the jokes, or maybe are inspired to give ultra running a go.

What's important to remember with ultras is that all things are relative. Everyone who runs 100 miles had once never run 5k. Remember that. I was able to complete the ONER because I built up to it, but a couple of the participants had never run more than a marathon before and still made it to the end. As with most things in life two of the most important ingredients in making it happen are wanting to and believing you can. Before my ankle injury flared up at Caesar's Camp I'd started to let negative thoughts creep in, and everything seemed a lot harder as a result. This doesn't mean if you think positively then everything will always go your way, because I've seen countless times that this simply isn't true, but I definitely think that believing something can be done increases the likelihood that it will be.

Now let's talk about eating. Simply because one of the questions I often get asked is whether I have a strict diet if I run ultramarathons. The answer is that no, I don't have a particularly strict diet at all. I was vegetarian for 16 years, from the age of 16, but now I'm not. I can't say whether or not it's a coincidence but shortly before going to the Isles of Scilly I was bitten by a spider I was trying to rescue. I couldn't believe it. For some time afterwards I would tell anyone who would listen that a spider had bitten me. When on the Isles of Scilly Boldebort bought a sausage roll one day, and as soon as she took it out of the bag I really craved it. I told her, and she offered me a bite. I didn't like it, but then I started craving more meat. Within a week or two I was a full blown meat eater again. I'd always been a vegetarian because I didn't like meat, but now I did. So I ate it. I must say it's made my life a little bit easier, because now wherever I go there's likely to be at least something I can eat. Just as with that bar in Port St. John's that sold only alcoholic drinks, there are numerous places that don't have a vegetarian option. Now it's no problem.

I do try to eat healthily. I'm making more and more effort to avoid processed foods as much as possible, but when you don't have a lot of money it's difficult to do this all the time. Also when you like crisps as much as I do. And chocolate cakes. Of course you can make alternatives using only natural ingredients, but to be frank I don't have the time most days. I'm hoping in the future I will have the time. In the future I'm hoping to eat mostly natural food but still to treat myself now and then. A number of ultra runners are extremely particular about their diet. Scott Jurek won many big races on a vegan diet, and Mike Arnstein has done pretty well on fruitarian diet, but personally I'm not really sure how they do it. I just love dairy too much, and don't love fruit enough. I do love making juices with various fruit and vegetables, but I couldn't make it my entire diet. My personal belief is that eating natural foods, and a good balance of them, is the way forward. If you disagree I don't want to argue about it. You eat what you like, and please let me do the same.

Ok, so I've talked about money, God, eating and running. So what's left? Well, mostly things that I don't particularly want to talk about to the whole world. Some things must remain private. That is why I've not named a number of people I've talked about in this book. I like to think I've not made anyone seem dreadful, but I do still want to protect peoples' privacy.

I guess a few final words on the Isles of Scilly. I hope to spend a fair bit more time there one way or the other. If I manage to make enough money to go and live there then great. If not then there'll be plenty more holidays I hope. I couldn't go there without Boldebort and her son, as that would be like going for the most exquisite curry you will ever taste without inviting the only other people who love curry as much as you. We'll have to go on the plane though, because the first time we went we took the boat, as it was cheaper, but poor Boldebort spent almost the entire voyage in a state of perpetual vomitation. Seeing as she has emetophobia this was a far from ideal situation for her, and I can still see the distraught expression on her face that seemed to say "Please make it stop," "How could this be happening?" and "I'm sorry you have to hold this sick bag for me. You are the best" all at the same time. As soon as she got off the boat on the other side she felt Ok, but she still talks of that sea crossing often, and it clearly left a mark on her. For the record I wasn't sick at all, and her son only was a little bit. I have never been seasick, and perhaps this is something that is also connected to my pirate ancestry. On the voyage on the way back the seas were a lot calmer, and nobody was sick. Hooray.

Now, about coincidences. On that sea voyage on the way back from the Isles of Scilly we were playing a game of I Spy. I had one beginning with 'S' and Boldebort said "Stog", looking at a dog across the deck. We laughed and thought no more about it, apart from saying "Stog. Hahahahaha" quite a few more times. Anyway, a couple of weeks later we were looking through some photos from the holiday and reminisced about the 'stog' incident. Literally a minute later we were stunned into silence when we saw the word 'Stogs' on a banner in one of the photos. It turns out that Betty Stogs is a Cornish Ale. Neither of us had ever heard of it, and Boldebort happened to say "Stog" about an hour before we were underneath a banner advertising Betty Stogs. What???

Coincidences seem to follow us around. Another day we were in Charmouth and I said "I really want to do that," talking I think about going to the Isles of Scilly as it happens, just as some young girls were walking the other way and one of them said "I really don't want to do that," talking about something completely different. Or perhaps it was about the same thing, who knows? The most amazing coincidence ever though was when I was travelling in South Africa I met a guy known as Botswana Dave, because he was originally from Botswana, who had gone to the same Uni as me at the same time and known a number of the same people but we'd not known each other. I met him in a place called Wilderness. The only other time I've seen him since was at Heathrow Airport when I'd just got back from Cuba and he was just about to go to Botswana. What's more, I'd been telling Libby the walk leader about him just a few days before, and seeing as she was standing right next to me I was able to say "You know that guy I was telling you about who I met in Wilderness? This is him." Was pretty handy, because I could prove my first amazing coincidence story wasn't made up, and now I had an even better one.

I feel like I should end this by saying something incredibly profound. Something that will inspire you to do something amazing, or perhaps something that will move you to tears. However, that's not really my style I'm afraid. It would be more in keeping with my personality to end this with something a bit silly. I'm still undecided as to which I will go for, but while I make my mind up let me ask you something. Once on a bottle of shower gel I saw the phrase 'Intensely relaxing.' Now, isn't this an oxymoron? I thought the whole point of relaxation was that it isn't meant to be intense. I thought it was meant to be a break from the intensity of modern life. Or am I so out of touch with the youth nowadays that I didn't realise the quality of relaxation is measured by the level of its intensity?

I know not. I know not how to end this book either, except by including my old poem 'Love is a Barely Seaworthy Fishing Boat' in its entirety. So I will.

My heart was trampled on by a rhinocerous or two

And thrown up in the air into the beak of a waiting heron

The heron dropped it onto the pavement

Then a few hours later it was midday and the heat from the sun became a little too intense

My heart began to steam and the steam of my happiness was evaporated into the atmosphere

Into the path of a waiting raincloud

Then it rained down at great velocity onto the road

Those tears of happiness of mine made quite an impact when they landed

And then the rain it went away but my happiness was liquid and the road was on a fairly steep gradient

So my happiness flowed down towards a manhole then it dripped into the sewer and you can guess it wasn't very pleasant down there

That's why you should never put your happiness in someone else's hands

Your happiness is like an egg and sooner or later that person will

Forget it's there and make a fist out of their hand

And the shell will crack and the yolk will run between their fingers

And if you're lucky they might think to themselves 'What have I done?'

At least if they regret their actions you can pretend it was their loss

But it'll still be really rather miserable

My heart was taken out to sea in a barely seaworthy fishing boat with a crew who really had no idea what they were doing

And I bet you know where this is going next but actually that bit was just a dream and my heart woke up in a garden

Twenty years went by and the grass grew very tall and blocked out the sun, and so my heart grew ever colder

Several generations of sparrows came and went but never did one of them look my heart in the eye

Which it didn't even have

Because it was a heart

But not one of those unkind sparrows ever acknowledged my heart's existence

And as I'm sure you can imagine

That wasn't very nice

That's why you should never put your happiness in someone else's hands

Your happiness is like an egg and sooner or later that person will

Forget it's there and open up their hand

And the egg will fall and splatter on the ground

That's why whenever someone tells you that they love you

They might as well be telling you that one day they'll destroy you

So don't let anyone get close to you or if you must

Prepare to find yourself in my position

Masking all your pain with a quite preposterous poem that doesn't make a lot of sense

To anyone except for yourself

But if somebody, just one person smiles when they hear your poem

Then that just adds insult to injury because your heartbreak is comical to them

So if you laughed at anything in this poem

I hope you're proud of yourself

I bet if you saw someone crying you'd just point and laugh

And take a picture on your phone for all your friends to see

And because life is so unfair despite all this being true

The woman I love would be in love with you instead of me

So there you have it. That was the poem. I hope you enjoyed it, but the real reason I included it here was to say that it's a measure of how much I've changed as a person since I originally wrote it that it now feels like it was written by somebody else. Make of that what you will. That's what book endings are for, right?

Further Reading

Now, I thought it would be wrong of me to mention some of the fabulous ultra runners I have in this book without providing links to some of their blogs. Here are a selection of those I follow myself that I would not hesitate to recommend if running is your thing: -

www.robbiebritton.co.uk – Robbie's highly entertaining blog can be found here, as well as how to go about hiring him as a coach if you enjoy pain and/or want to become the best ultra runner you can be.

www.constantforwardmotion.blogspot.co.uk – Sam Robson's latest musings and running tales with the occasional product review. Always humorous and thought-provoking.

www.marvellousmimi.com/v2/category/blog – If you're already feeling that your running achievements are leaving a little to be desired then Mimi Anderson's blog is not going to make you feel any better, but if you want awe inspiring reading then there's arguably no better place to go.

www.runningandstuff.com – If you're worried that you can't achieve amazing things in ultra running whilst eating whatever you like whenever you like and being proud of it then James Adams' blog is the one for you. On a serious note, James' achievements are stunning. He has run across America, completed Spartathlon three times and many other tough races both in the UK and abroad. He is not just well known in ultra circles for his sarcasm.

www.ultraavon.com – Paul Ali, at the time of writing, has completed every ultra race he's started, including the 250 mile Thames Ring, a 24-hour race, Spartathlon, Caesar's Camp 100 and the Winter 100. None of these have been in fancy dress, but a number of others have that he's completed. He also compiles an online magazine, Ultra Tales. A massively popular character on the UK ultra scene.

And a few books:

Dead Man Running: From Alcohol to Atacama by Billy Isherwood – Written very much in the author's own voice, this is an inspiring tale for me of how no matter how bad things seem there is always hope.

Nourishing Traditions by Sally Fallon – Really interesting read about how following a traditional diet of tribes throughout the world is far more beneficial than the modern diets most of us follow. One I hope to follow myself more in the future.

The Harry Potter series – I've read the first two at the time of writing, having avoided them for years. They're actually edge of seat stuff!

No Fixed Abode by Charlie Carroll – A really thought-provoking read about homelessness. It inspired me to think more about this issue. Maybe it will you too.